SANJEEV
KAPOOR

100 CHINESE RECIPES

EASY CHINESE HOME COOKING

IN ASSOCIATION WITH ALYONA KAPOOR

Popular Prakashan
www.popularprakashan.com

Published by
POPULAR PRAKASHAN PVT. LTD.
301, Mahalaxmi Chambers
22, Bhulabhai Desai Road
Mumbai – 400 026
www.popularprakashan.com

First Published 2017

(4465)
ISBN: 978-81-7991-906-4

Food Stylist: Afraz Sheikh
Photography: Siddharth Kotian
Part images (other than recipes) sourced from Shutterstock
Design: Devaki Bavkar

Printed in India
by Thomson Press (India) Ltd.
New Delhi

AUTHOR'S NOTE

It is not for nothing that Chinese cuisine enjoys the number one position amongst all the cuisines in the world today. It has been so for a number of years now. So what is it about Chinese food that makes it so very popular? The answer lies in the fact that it is wholesome, quite economical, balanced and simply delicious. It is also easy to cook and digest.

As an ancient Chinese proverb says, "A good meal is eaten first with the eyes, then with the nose and finally with the mouth." Each Chinese dish reflects a balance of taste, texture, aroma and colour. All the six basic flavours of sweet, sour, pungent, hot, salty and spicy are very well incorporated in all their dishes.

100 Chinese Recipes is sure to satiate the palate of all Chinese food lovers. These recipes are tasty, wholesome and simple to make with easily available ingredients. All the recipes in this book serve four portions. From soups to desserts, both vegetarian and non-vegetarian, this book has an extensive collection of recipes enabling you to cook a different dish each time you crave a Chinese meal.

Happy cooking!

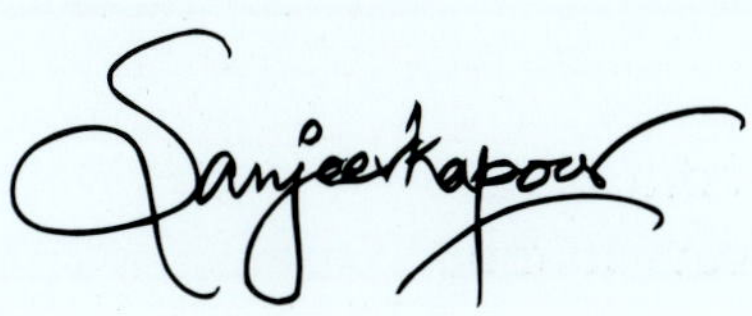

CONTENTS

Soups and Salads

001

HOT AND SOUR NOODLE SOUP

Ingredients

250 grams noodles
2 fresh red chillies, finely chopped
1 teaspoon vinegar
1 tablespoon oil
2 spring onions with greens, sliced separately
1 inch ginger, sliced
3 cups Vegetable Stock (page 159)
½ cup corn kernels
Salt to taste
⅓ cup cornflour slurry

Method

1. Heat sufficient water in a deep non-stick pan. Add the noodles and cook. Strain and set aside.
2. Heat the oil in a non-stick pan. Add the spring onion bulbs and ginger and sauté well.
3. Add the vegetable stock and corn kernels; stir well, bring to a boil and simmer.
4. Add the red chillies, mix and simmer. Add the salt and cornstarch slurry, mix well and bring to a boil.
5. Add the noodles along with the vinegar. Mix well and bring the mixture to a boil.
6. Add the spring onion greens, mix well and serve piping hot.

002

SWEETCORN LEMON CORIANDER SOUP

Ingredients

1 tin (420 gram) cream-style sweetcorn
2 lemons
¼ cup chopped fresh coriander
4½ cups Vegetable Stock (page 159)
2 inches lemongrass root, chopped
1 inch ginger, chopped
4-5 lemon leaves
Salt to taste
3 teaspoons cornflour
1 teaspoon vinegar
Lemon slices, for garnishing
A coriander sprig, for garnishing

Method

1. Heat four cups vegetable stock in a deep non-stick pan. Add lemongrass root, ginger and lemon leaves and let the mixture boil for three to four minutes.
2. Remove the lemongrass root, ginger and lemon leaves and add the cream-style sweetcorn and mix well. Add the salt and mix.
3. Mix the cornflour with the remaining vegetable stock till smooth and add to the soup. Mix well and cook till the soup thickens.
4. Add the chopped coriander and vinegar and mix well. Squeeze the juice of the lemons and mix.
5. Serve the soup piping hot garnished with the lemon slices and a coriander sprig.

003

VEGETABLE MANCHOW SOUP

Ingredients

1 medium carrot, chopped

¼ small cabbage, chopped

2-3 fresh button mushrooms, sliced

2-3 Chinese mushroom, soaked, drained and roughly chopped

½ medium green capsicum, chopped

2 tablespoons oil

1 spring onion, sliced

½ inch ginger, chopped

2-3 garlic cloves, chopped

4 cups Vegetable Stock (page 159)

2 green chillies

½ tablespoon red chilli sauce

2 tablespoons soy sauce

50 grams tofu (bean curd), cut into ½-inch cubes

2 inches bamboo shoot, cut into small pieces

3 teaspoons cornflour

Salt to taste

1 cup noodles, deep-fried

Sliced spring onion greens, for garnishing

Method

1. Heat the oil in a non-stick wok. Add the spring onion, ginger and garlic and toss.
2. Add the carrot, cabbage and button mushrooms and Chinese mushrooms.
3. Add the vegetable stock and green chillies. Add the red chilli sauce and soy sauce and mix. Add tofu and bamboo shoot and mix.
4. Mix the cornflour with one-fourth cup water and add to the soup and cook till it thickens. Add the salt and mix.
5. Add the capsicum, reserving some for garnish, and mix well.
6. Serve hot garnished with deep-fried noodles, reserved capsicum and spring onion greens.

004

HOT AND SOUR SOUP

Ingredients

4-6 French beans, stringed and finely chopped
4 fresh button mushrooms, sliced
½ medium carrot, grated
¼ small cabbage, finely chopped
1 tablespoon oil
1 small onion, finely chopped
1 inch ginger, chopped
2-3 garlic cloves, finely chopped
2 inches celery stalk, finely chopped
2 tablespoons soy sauce
2 tablespoons green chilli sauce
5 cups Vegetable Stock (page 159)
Salt to taste
½ teaspoon white pepper powder
½ teaspoon sugar
3 teaspoons cornflour
½ medium green capsicum, finely chopped
1 stalk spring onion greens, finely chopped
1 tablespoon white vinegar
Mixed capsicum curls, for garnishing
Spring onion green curls, for garnishing

Method

1. Heat the oil in a non-stick wok; add the onion, ginger and garlic and sauté till the onion is translucent. Add the celery, French beans, mushrooms, carrot and cabbage and sauté for two to three minutes.
2. Add the soy sauce and green chilli sauce and mix well. Add four and half cups stock, salt, pepper powder and sugar and mix.
3. Mix the cornflour with the remaining stock and add to the soup and mix well.
4. Add the capsicum and mix. Add the spring onion greens and vinegar and mix and remove from the heat.
5. Serve the soup piping hot garnished with mixed capsicum curls and spring onion green curls.

005

BEAN CURD EGG DROP SOUP

Ingredients

100 grams bean curd (tofu), cut into small cubes
2 eggs
3 cups Chicken Stock (page 159)
2 spring onions with greens
2 teaspoons cornflour
1 tablespoon light soy sauce
Salt to taste
Crushed black peppercorns to taste

Method

1. Chop the spring onion greens. Halve spring onion bulbs vertically and slice horizontally. Set aside.
2. Break eggs and separate the yolks and whites in two separate bowls. For this recipe use only the whites.
3. Mix cornflour with one-fourth cup water in a small bowl. Set aside.
4. Heat chicken stock in a non-stick wok. Add the spring onion bulbs.
5. Add bean curd along with light soy sauce, salt and crushed black peppercorns.
6. Add two tablespoons of cornflour mixture and mix.
7. Whisk the egg whites and add to the soup in a thin stream. The egg white will coagulate and rise to the top.
8. Add spring onion greens and mix. Serve piping hot.

006

TOMATO EGG SOUP

Ingredients

2-3 medium tomatoes, blanched and peeled
1 egg
4 cups Vegetable Stock (page 159)
Salt to taste
Black pepper powder to taste
3-4 spring onion bulbs, chopped
50 grams bean curd (tofu), chopped
½ teaspoon light soy sauce
1 stalk spring onion greens, chopped

Method

1. Break the egg into a bowl, add salt and black pepper powder and whisk lightly.
2. Heat a non-stick frying pan and pour the egg mixture into it. Rotate the pan so that the egg spreads evenly all around. Take the pan off the heat and carefully flip the omelette. Set aside.
3. Heat the vegetable stock in a deep non-stick pan.
4. Halve the tomatoes and remove seeds; chop and add to the stock in the pan. Add the spring onion bulbs and mix.
5. Add the bean curd, salt and soy sauce and mix.
6. Add the spring onion greens to the soup and let it simmer for two to three minutes.
7. Roll the omelette into a cylinder and cut into thin rings. Put these slices into a serving bowl.
8. Pour the soup over the omelette rings and serve the soup piping hot.

007

CHICKEN NOODLE SOUP

Ingredients

300 grams rice noodles
2 tablespoons fish sauce
2 tablespoons soy sauce
2 fresh red chillies, seeded and sliced
1 medium onion, sliced
1¼ cups bean sprouts, blanched
2 tablespoons chopped fresh coriander
10-12 fresh basil, torn
White pepper powder to taste
1 lemon, cut into wedges

Broth

500 grams boneless chicken, cut into cubes
10 cups Chicken Stock (page 159)
4 spring onions, sliced
1 inch ginger, crushed
1 inch cinnamon stick
Salt to taste
2 teaspoons sugar

Method

1. For the broth, pour the chicken stock into a deep non-stick pan and heat. Add the chicken cubes, spring onions, ginger, cinnamon, salt and sugar. Stir well and simmer for forty to forty-five minutes. Remove the scum which rises to the surface at short intervals.
2. Strain the stock and set aside. Cut the chicken cubes into small pieces. Set aside.
3. Add the fish sauce to the strained stock and mix. Set aside.
4. Boil four cups water in another deep non-stick pan and soak the rice noodles in it. Strain the noodles into a bowl and add a little cold water to it.
5. Mix the soy sauce and chillies in a bowl. Set aside.

6. Divide the noodles equally into four serving bowl. Place the chicken pieces over them along with onion, beans sprouts, chopped coriander, fresh basil and pepper powder. Pour the stock over. Drizzle a little of the chilli-in-soy sauce, garnish with a lemon wedge and serve immediately.

008

CHICKEN BROTH WITH POACHED EGG

Ingredients

400 grams boneless chicken, boiled and shredded

4 cups Chicken Stock (page 159)

4 eggs

1 tablespoon oil

1½ inches ginger, chopped

12-14 garlic cloves, chopped

2 medium carrots, peeled and cut into thick strips

1 medium cabbage, cut into thick strips

Salt to taste

1 teaspoon crushed black peppercorns

4 teaspoons soy sauce

2 teaspoons red chilli sauce

3 stalks spring onion greens, finely chopped

Method

1. Heat the oil in a non-stick pan. Add the ginger and garlic and sauté well.
2. Add the carrots and sauté. Add the cabbage, mix and sauté further.
3. Add the salt, crushed peppercorns, soy sauce and red chilli sauce. Mix well and add chicken stock along with the chicken. Mix well, cover and cook till the vegetables are done.
4. Break one egg each in individual bowls.
5. Transfer the cooked vegetables and chicken equally into four serving bowls. Continue to boil the stock.
6. Slide in the eggs, into the boiling stock and poach them, one by one. Reserve the stock.
7. Sprinkle the spring onion greens equally into the serving bowls, reserving some for garnishing. Pour the reserved stock over them.Top each bowl with a poached egg, garnish with the reserved spring onion greens and serve immediately.

009

PRAWN BALL SOUP

Ingredients

250 grams prawns, shelled and deveined

1 tablespoon oil

1 inch ginger, sliced

5-6 medium fresh button mushrooms, sliced

3-4 slices tinned bamboo shoots, boiled for 10-15 minutes, drained and chopped

4 cups Chicken Stock (page 159)

Salt to taste

Black pepper powder to taste

1 tablespoon cornflour

1 egg white

10-12 fresh spinach leaves

5-6 black peppercorns, crushed

2-3 stalks spring onion greens chopped

Method

1. Heat the oil in a non-stick pan. Add the ginger and sauté for a minute.
2. Add the mushrooms and bamboo shoots and sauté for a minute. Add the chicken stock and bring the mixture to a boil.
3. Grind the prawns with the salt and pepper powder to a fine paste. Transfer prawn paste into a bowl, add the cornflour and egg white and mix well.
4. Drop in small portions of prawn paste with a spoon into the boiling stock and cook till the prawn balls are done.
5. Tear the spinach leaves and add to soup and stir lightly. Add the salt and crushed peppercorns and mix.
6. Add the spring onion greens, mix well and cook for two minutes.
7. Serve piping hot.

010

SWEETCORN CRABMEAT SOUP

Ingredients

2½ cups cream-style sweetcorn
3 tablespoons cooked crabmeat
3 cups Chicken Stock (page 159)
2 tablespoons cornflour
Salt to taste
½ teaspoon white pepper powder
1 tablespoon sugar
2 egg whites
1 teaspoon red chilli sauce
Spring onion greens strips, for garnishing
Red capsicum curls, for garnishing

Method

1. Bring the chicken stock to a boil in a deep non-stick pan.
2. Mix the cornflour with one-fourth cup water till smooth. Set aside.
3. Mix the salt, white pepper powder, half tablespoon sugar and a little water in a bowl. Set aside.
4. Add the cream-style corn to the boiling stock and mix well. Add the sugar-pepper mixture and the cornflour mixture. Mix well and cook for two to three minutes.
5. Adjust the salt and add the remaining sugar. Mix well and cook till the mixture comes to a boil.
6. Beat the egg whites and add. Mix well.
7. Add the crabmeat and red chilli sauce and mix again. Cook for one minute.
8. Serve piping hot garnished with the spring onion greens strips and red capsicum curls.

011

VEGETABLE RIBBONS

Ingredients

1 medium yellow zucchini, trimmed
1 medium green zucchini, trimmed
2 medium carrots, trimmed
2 medium cucumbers, trimmed
Salt to taste
3-4 fresh basil for garnishing

Dressing
Salt to taste
¼ teaspoon red chilli flakes
1 teaspoon brown sugar
1 tablespoon soy sauce
2 tablespoons vinegar

Method

1. Peel the zucchinis, carrots and cucumbers lengthwise into thin ribbons with the help of a potato peeler or a manual slicer. Place the ribbons on a plate and sprinkle a little salt. Set aside for five minutes.
2. To make the dressing, mix the salt, red chilli flakes, brown sugar, soy sauce and vinegar in a bowl.
3. Arrange the vegetable ribbons on a plate and sprinkle the dressing on them. Serve garnished with fresh basil.

012

CHILLI BEAN SALAD WITH CARAMELISED WALNUTS

Ingredients

150 grams long beans, cut into long strips and blanched

150 grams French beans, cut into long strips and blanched

Toasted white sesame seeds, for sprinkling

Toasted black sesame seeds, for sprinkling

Caramelised Walnuts

150 grams walnut kernels, blanched

75 grams sugar

2 tablespoons honey

Oil for deep-frying

Dressing

6-8 pickled jalapeños, roughly chopped

2 tablespoons red chilli sauce

1 tablespoon Sichuan chutney

Method

1. For the caramelised walnuts, heat one-fourth cup water in a non-stick pan; add sugar and honey and mix well. Add blanched walnut kernels and bring to a boil. Drain the nuts.
2. Heat sufficient oil in a wok. Deep-fry the walnut kernels in hot oil till crisp. Drain on absorbent paper.
3. To make dressing, mix jalapeños, red chilli sauce and Sichuan chutney in a bowl.
4. Mix both the beans in a large bowl; add the dressing and mix well.
5. Arrange the beans on a serving platter, sprinkle white and black sesame seeds, top with caramelised walnuts and serve immediately.

013

CHINESE-STYLE EGG SALAD

Ingredients

6 eggs, hard boiled

2 teaspoons tea leaves

1 star anise

1 inch cinnamon stick

1 tablespoon soy sauce

3-4 spring onion bulbs, cut into diamond shapes

3-4 lettuce leaves

Sesame oil, for drizzling

Toasted sesame seeds, for sprinkling

Dressing

2 tablespoons mayonnaise

2 teaspoons red chilli sauce

Juice of ½ lemon

Method

1. Boil two cups water in a deep non-stick pan. Add the tea leaves, star anise, cinnamon stick and soy sauce and mix well.
2. Roughly crack the shells of the eggs with the back of a spoon and add to the pan. Cover and cook for thirty-five to forty minutes. Remove from the heat and leave the eggs in this water overnight or for three to four hours. Drain the water.
3. Peel the eggs and transfer them into a bowl. Wash the eggs in normal water to remove the shells completely.
4. For the dressing, mix the mayonnaise, red chilli sauce and lemon juice in a bowl.
5. Roughly tear the lettuce leaves into another bowl. Add the spring onion bulbs and mix well. Make a bed of the mixture on a serving platter and pour the dressing over it.
6. Cut the eggs into four pieces and place on the lettuce leaves. Drizzle the sesame oil, sprinkle the sesame seeds and serve immediately.

014

GLASS NOODLES AND EGG STIR-FRY

Method

1. Break eggs into a bowl; add salt, chilli powder and whisk together. Add two tablespoons water and whisk again.
2. Heat two tablespoons oil in a non-stick pan; add half the egg mixture and rotate the pan so that the egg spreads evenly. Cover and cook till done. Transfer to a plate. Cook the remaining egg similarly. Tightly roll the omelettes and cut into one-fourth-inch wide slices. Set aside.
3. Heat two tablespoons oil in the same pan; add spring onions and sauté.
4. Add garlic and sauté. Add carrot, cabbage, capsicum, soy sauce and stir-fry for two to three minutes.
5. Heat sufficient water in a deep non-stick pan.
6. Arrange the noodles in a bowl and pour the hot water over them till they get soaked completely.
7. Drain the noodles and add to the vegetables and mix well.
8. Transfer the mixture into a serving bowl. Arrange the omelette over them and serve hot.

Ingredients

200 grams glass noodles

2 eggs

Salt to taste

¼ teaspoon red chilli powder

4 tablespoons oil

3 spring onion bulbs, sliced

1 tablespoon chopped garlic

1 medium carrot, grated

½ medium cabbage, shredded

1 medium green capsicum, cut into thin strips

1 teaspoon soy sauce

Snacks and Starters

015

HONEY CHILLI PANEER

Ingredients

For One Portion

250 grams cottage cheese, cut into 1-inch cubes

2 tablespoons honey

2 teaspoons red chilli paste

1 tablespoon red chilli flakes

4 tablespoons oil

2 medium onions, cut into thick slices

2 medium green capsicums, cut into thick strips

2 medium green capsicums, cut into thick strips

Salt to taste

5-6 garlic cloves, chopped

1 teaspoon ginger paste

2 tablespoons sweet chilli sauce

3 teaspoon cornflour mixed with 4 tablespoons water

2 teaspoons vinegar

Method

1. Heat two tablespoons oil in a non-stick wok. Add the onions, capsicums and salt and sauté, tossing, for two to three minutes. Transfer into a bowl.
2. Heat the remaining oil in the same wok; add the garlic and ginger paste and sauté. Add the sweet chilli sauce, red chilli paste and salt and mix. Add half cup water and mix. Add the cornflour mixture and mix and cook till the sauce thickens slightly.
3. Add the cottage cheese and mix gently. Add the chilli flakes and one tablespoon honey and mix. Add the vinegar and mix again. Adjust the seasoning.
4. Heat a sizzler plate. Place the sizzler plate on its wooden base.
5. Spread the capsicum-onion mixture on the base. Top with the cottage cheese mixture. Drizzle the remaining honey over it and serve immediately

Image on the opposite page

016

STEAMED BROCCOLI WITH THREE SEEDS

Ingredients

1 medium broccoli, separated into florets
1 tablespoon pumpkin seeds
1 tablespoon sunflower seeds
1 tablespoon sesame seeds
A few pak choi leaves
2 teaspoons oyster sauce
2 teaspoons red chilli sauce
1 teaspoon finely chopped ginger

Method

1. Heat three to four cups water in a deep non-stick pan.
2. Dry-roast the pumpkin seeds, sunflower seeds and sesame seeds, in a non-stick pan, till fragrant and transfer into a bowl. Set aside.
3. Place the pak choi leaves in a bamboo steamer. Place the broccoli florets over the pak choi leaves in the steamer; close the lid and place it in the boiling water. Steam till the broccoli is soft.
4. Heat the oyster sauce in a non-stick pan. Add the chilli sauce and three teaspoons water and mix. Add the ginger, mix well, cook for two minutes and remove from heat.
5. Transfer the broccoli florets onto a serving dish. Drizzle the prepared sauce on top and sprinkle the three seed mixture.
6. Serve immediately.

017

BABY CORN SALT AND PEPPER

Ingredients

16-20 baby corns
2 tablespoons cornflour
Salt to taste
7-8 black peppercorns, crushed
2 tablespoons oil + for deep-frying
4 spring onions with greens, diagonally sliced
4 inches celery stalk, chopped
2 green chillies, sliced
1 inch ginger, chopped
3-4 garlic cloves, chopped

Method

1. Parboil the baby corns. Drain and slice them diagonally. Transfer them into a bowl; add the cornflour, salt and half the crushed peppercorns and mix well.
2. Heat sufficient oil in a wok and deep-fry the baby corn slices till golden. Drain on absorbent paper.
3. Heat two tablespoons oil in a non-stick wok. Add the spring onions, celery, green chillies, ginger and garlic and sauté for two minutes. Add the baby corns, salt and the remaining crushed peppercorns and sauté for a minute.
4. Serve hot.

018

CHILLI TOFU

Ingredients

500 grams bean curd (tofu), cut into 1-inch cubes

1 tablespoon green chilli sauce

3 green chillies, cut into thin long slices

4 tablespoons oil

2 teaspoons chopped ginger

2 teaspoons chopped garlic

4 tablespoons dark soy sauce

1 medium onion, quartered and layers separated

1 medium green capsicum, cut into 1-inch pieces

Salt to taste

¼ teaspoon black pepper powder

3-4 tablespoons cornflour, mixed in ¼ cup water

2 tablespoons vinegar

1 stalk spring onion greens, cut into 1-inch pieces

Method

1. Heat the oil in a non-stick wok; add the tofu and sauté, tossing, for five minutes. Drain on an absorbent paper and transfer into a bowl and set aside.
2. Add the ginger and garlic to the oil remaining in the wok and sauté till fragrant. Add the soy sauce and green chilli sauce and mix. Add the onion and green chillies and mix. Add the green capsicum and mix.
3. Add the salt, pepper powder and half cup water and mix.
4. Add the cornflour mixture and mix.
5. Add the tofu and mix. Add the vinegar and spring onion greens and mix.
6. Serve hot.

019

FRIED TOFU IN CHILLI SOY SAUCE

Ingredients

200 grams bean curd (tofu), cut into thick slices

2 green chillies, roughly chopped

2 bird's eye chillies, roughly chopped

2 tablespoons dark soy sauce

1 tablespoon oil + for deep-frying

3-4 garlic cloves, crushed

7-8 shallots, sliced

4 tablespoons palm sugar

Salt to taste

1 teaspoon vinegar

¼ medium red capsicum, cut into triangles

¼ medium green capsicum, cut into triangles

Bean sprouts for garnishing

Method

1. To make the chilli soy sauce, heat one tablespoon oil in a non-stick pan; add the garlic and shallots and sauté till translucent. Add the dark soy sauce, palm sugar and salt and mix well. Let the sugar melt. Add the green chillies, bird's eye chillies and two tablespoons water and mix well. Cook till the sauce thickens.
2. Add the vinegar to the sauce in the pan and mix well. Simmer for a minute. Set aside.
3. Heat sufficient oil in a kadai. Add the tofu and deep-fry till crisp and brown from all sides. Drain on absorbent paper. Cut the fried tofu into small cubes.
4. Flash-fry capsicum in the same hot oil in the kadai. Drain on absorbent paper.
5. Place the fried tofu cubes and capsicum pieces in a serving plate.
6. Pour the prepared sauce over the fried tofu and capsicums, garnish with the bean sprouts and serve immediately.

020

NOODLE PILLOWS

Ingredients

150 grams glass noodles
4-5 cabbage leaves
1 tablespoon oil
1 medium onion, finely chopped
4-5 button mushrooms, sliced
½ cup grated carrot
1½ tablespoons Sichuan sauce
½ cup cooked rice
Salt to taste
1 tablespoon cornflour slurry
1 banana leaf

Method

1. Heat one cup water in a non-stick pan; add the cabbage leaves and boil till leaves become soft. Remove the leaves and place in two cups cold water.
2. Heat oil in non-stick wok; add the onion and sauté till translucent.
3. Add the mushrooms and carrot and mix well. Add one tablespoon Sichuan sauce and mix well. Cook till the excess water begins to evaporate.
4. Add the glass noodles and mix well. Add the rice and the remaining Sichuan sauce and mix well. Add two to three tablespoons water and mix well. Add the salt and mix well. Add the cornflour slurry and mix well. Remove from heat when the sauce becomes thick. Set aside.
5. Wipe dry the cabbage leaves with absorbent paper to remove the extra moisture. Place a portion of noodle stuffing in centre of each leaf and fold to make pillows.
6. Place a banana leaf in a bamboo steamer and make a few small slits on it with the tip of a knife.
7. Heat sufficient water in a non-stick wok; place the bamboo steamer in it, place the noodle pillows over the banana leaf, cover with a lid and steam for eight to ten minutes.
8. Remove the noodle pillows from the steamer, arrange on a serving platter and serve immediately

021

SICHUAN CHEESE FRITTERS

Ingredients

1 cup grated processed cheese
2 teaspoons Sichuan sauce
½ cup refined flour
Oil for deep-frying
1 teaspoon soda bicarbonate
1 cup chopped onions
¼ cup chopped spring onions
1 tablespoon chopped garlic
Salt to taste
Buttermilk, as required
Red chilli sauce, as required
Fresh parsley, for garnishing

Method

1. Place the grated cheese in a bowl; add the refined flour, soda bicarbonate, onions, spring onions, garlic, Sichuan sauce, salt and sufficient buttermilk and mix to make a soft dough.
2. Heat sufficient oil in a wok.
3. Shape the mixture into quenelles with two teaspoons, slide into hot oil and deep-fry till golden and crisp. Drain on absorbent paper.
4. Put a little red chilli sauce in a small plate. Place the fritters over the sauce, garnish with a little parsley and serve hot.

022

STEAMED MOMOS

Ingredients

1 cup refined flour

2 tablespoons oil

2 spring onions, finely chopped

1 inch ginger, finely chopped

1 green chilli, finely chopped

4-5 fresh button mushrooms, finely chopped

10 French beans, finely chopped

1 medium carrot, finely chopped

1 stalk spring onion greens, chopped

¼ cup bean sprouts

Salt to taste

8-10 black peppercorns, crushed

½ tablespoon light soy sauce

1 tablespoon cornflour

A few cabbage leaves

1 teaspoon sesame oil

Method

1. Mix the refined flour with five tablespoons of water and knead into a soft dough. Cover with a moist piece of muslin and set aside for fifteen minutes.
2. Heat the oil in a non-stick wok. Add the spring onions, ginger and green chilli and sauté. And the mushrooms, French beans, carrot, spring onion greens, bean sprouts, salt, crushed peppercorns and soy sauce and mix well.
3. Add the cornflour mixed in one-fourth cup water. Cook till the sauce thickens. Remove from the heat and cool.
4. Divide the dough into small balls. Dust the balls in the flour and roll into small puris keeping the edges thin and the centre thick. Place a portion of stuffing in the centre of each puri, fold one end over the other and give it a half-moon shape.
5. Heat water in a deep non-stick pan. Line a bamboo basket with the cabbage leaves. Apply a little sesame oil on the momos and place them over the cabbage leaves. Cover the basket and place it over the hot water, cover the pan and steam for eight to ten minutes or till done.
6. Uncover the pan, take the basket out and open it. Serve the momos hot.

023

STIR-FRIED TOFU

Ingredients

200 grams bean curd (tofu), cut into ½-inch cubes

4 tablespoons oil

2 inches lemongrass root, thinly sliced

1 medium onion, diced and layers separated

2 medium green capsicums, cut into ½-inch pieces

1 tablespoon chopped garlic

1 teaspoon grated ginger

4-5 kaffir lime leaves

½ cup Coconut Milk (page 159)

Salt to taste

6-8 fresh Thai basil leaves

1 tablespoon sweet chilli sauce

1 teaspoon toasted onion seeds

Method

1. Heat the oil in a non-stick wok. Add the tofu and shallow-fry till golden. Drain on absorbent paper. Transfer on the work top and cut each cube diagonally to make triangles. Transfer them into a bowl.
2. Drain the excess oil, leaving two tablespoons, from the wok. Add the lemongrass root and sauté.
3. Add the onion, capsicums, garlic, ginger and kaffir lime leaves and toss.
4. Add the tofu, coconut milk and salt and mix. Add the fresh basil leaves and mix. Add the sweet chilli sauce, mix well and let it get heated through.
5. Transfer into a serving bowl, sprinkle toasted onion seeds and serve hot.

Note: To make the Stir-fried Tofu a bit spicier, add one-fourth teaspoon fresh red chilli.

024

SWEET POTATOES WITH HONEY

Ingredients

2 sweet potatoes
1½ teaspoons honey
3 tablespoons oil + for deep-frying
Salt to taste
½ teaspoon sugar
¼ teaspoon black pepper powder
1 teaspoon red chilli powder
2 tablespoons finely chopped garlic
4 spring onion bulbs, sliced
½ teaspoon soy sauce

Method

1. Scrub and wash sweet potatoes well. Cut them into four-inch pieces, halve them and cut into thin long strips. Transfer them into a bowl; drizzle one tablespoon oil, sprinkle salt, sugar, a pinch of black pepper powder and half teaspoon chilli powder and mix well.
2. Heat sufficient oil in a wok. Slide the strips into the hot oil and deep-fry till light brown. Drain on absorbent paper.
3. Heat two tablespoons oil in a non-stick pan; add the garlic and sauté till light brown.
4. Add the spring onions and sauté till the onions soften. Add the fried sweet potatoes and toss.
5. Add the remaining black pepper powder, remaining chilli powder, soy sauce and toss well. Add the honey and toss.
6. Transfer into a serving platter and serve hot.

025

VEGETABLE SPRING ROLLS

Ingredients

- 2 medium carrots, cut into thin strips
- 1 medium green capsicum, cut into thin strips
- ½ small cabbage, finely shredded
- 10 spring roll wrappers
- 2 tablespoons oil + for deep-frying
- 1 medium onion, thinly sliced
- 2 spring onions, thinly sliced
- Salt to taste
- ¼ teaspoon white pepper powder
- 1 tablespoon soy sauce
- ¾ cup bean sprouts
- 2 stalks spring onion greens, chopped
- 1 tablespoon cornflour

Method

1. To make the stuffing, heat two tablespoons oil in a non-stick wok. Add the onion, spring onions, carrots, capsicum, cabbage and salt and toss.
2. Add white pepper powder and soy sauce and mix. Add the bean sprouts and spring onion greens and mix. Cook till the vegetables soften. Remove the wok from the heat and set aside to cool.
3. Make a paste of cornflour with water. Set aside.
4. Spread the spring roll wrappers on the work top. Divide the stuffing into ten portions and place a portion on one side of each wrapper. Fold in the edges and roll tightly. Seal the open end with the cornflour paste. Keep the rolls under a moist piece of muslin if made much before deep-frying.
5. Heat sufficient oil in a wok. Gently slide the spring rolls into the hot oil and deep-fry till golden and crisp. Drain on absorbent paper.
6. Cut into smaller pieces and serve.

026

STIR-FRIED PAK CHOI

Ingredients

2-4 medium bunches pak choi
1 tablespoon oil
1 tablespoon crushed garlic
1 teaspoon soy sauce
1 teaspoon fish sauce
1 tablespoon oyster sauce
1 tablespoon sweet chilli sauce

Method

1. Separate the leaves of pak choi.
2. Heat the oil in a non-stick pan; add the garlic and sauté for half minute. Add the pak choi leaves and four to five tablespoons water, mix well and cook for three to four minutes.
3. Add the soy sauce, fish sauce, oyster sauce and sweet chilli sauce and mix well. Cook till the pak choi is done.
4. Transfer into a serving dish and serve immediately.

027

ASIAN LETTUCE WRAP WITH CHICKEN

Ingredients

2 bunches iceberg lettuce, separated into individual leaves
100 grams minced chicken
1 tablespoon olive oil
1 medium onion, chopped
1 tablespoon grated ginger
1 tablespoon chopped garlic
Salt to taste
1 tablespoon dark soy sauce
2 teaspoons Hoisin sauce
2 teaspoons sweet chilli sauce
1 medium carrot, grated
1 medium cucumber, finely chopped

Method

1. Heat the olive oil in a non-stick pan; add the onion, ginger and garlic and sauté for one to two minutes.
2. Add the chicken and continue to sauté. Add the salt, dark soy sauce, Hoisin sauce and sweet chilli sauce and mix. Cook till the chicken is done. Transfer into a bowl.
3. To make the wraps, place some chicken mixture in the centre of each lettuce leaf, top with the carrot and cucumber, roll the lettuce and serve.
4. Alternatively, serve the lettuce leaves, chicken mixture, carrot and cucumber separately so that each person can make their own rolls.

Ingredients

1 small broccoli, separated into florets and blanched

1 cup minced chicken

4 spring roll sheets

1 tablespoon oil + for deep-frying

1 tablespoon finely chopped garlic

1 medium onion, finely chopped

Salt to taste

Black pepper powder to taste

1 teaspoon soy sauce

2 tablespoons grated processed cheese

Refined flour paste, for sealing

A few fresh coriander sprigs, for garnishing

Sweet chilli sauce, to serve

028

BROCCOLI CHICKEN SPRING ROLLS

Method

1. Heat one tablespoon oil in a non-stick pan; add the garlic and sauté.
2. Add the onion and sauté for a minute. Add the minced chicken, salt and pepper powder and mix well. Add the soy sauce, mix well and cook for a while.
3. Roughly chop the blanched broccoli florets and add to the pan. Mix well and cook further till the chicken is done. Remove from heat and cool down to room temperature.
4. Add the cheese to the cooked mixture and mix well.
5. Place a spring roll sheet on a worktop. Put a generous spoonful of chicken mixture in the centre and spread a little. Roll the sheet tightly, sealing the edges with flour paste. Similarly make remaining spring rolls.
6. Heat sufficient oil in a wok. Deep-fry the spring rolls till golden and crisp. Drain on absorbent paper.
7. Halve the spring rolls and place on a serving plate. Garnish with a few coriander sprigs and serve hot with the sweet chilli sauce.

029

CHICKEN PARCELS

Ingredients

1 boneless chicken breast, cut into small cubes
4 white bread slices
2 tablespoons oil + for deep-frying
2 medium onions, chopped
2 tablespoons chopped garlic
1 tablespoon chopped ginger
Salt to taste
½ teaspoon crushed black peppercorns
2 green chillies, chopped
3 tablespoons roasted and skinned peanuts, crushed
2 teaspoons lemon juice

Method

1. Heat two tablespoons oil in a non-stick pan; add the onions, garlic and ginger and sauté.
2. Add the chicken, salt and crushed peppercorns and sauté for two minutes. Cover and cook for two minutes.
3. Add the green chillies and mix. Cover and cook till the chicken is done. Transfer into a bowl.
4. Add the crushed peanuts and lemon juice to the chicken and mix well.
5. Pour water into another bowl. Trim the edges of the bread slices and moisten them in water. Squeeze out the extra water by pressing the slices between your palms.
6. Place some chicken mixture in the centre of each slice, bring in the edges and shape into an oval croquette.
7. Heat sufficient oil in a kadai.
8. Slide the chicken parcels into the hot oil and deep-fry till golden and crisp. Drain on absorbent paper.
9. Serve hot garnished with round slices of onion, thin strips of green capsicums and a fresh red chilli flower.

030

CHILLI WINGS

Method

1. Place the chicken wings in a bowl; add the salt, chilli powder and lemon juice and mix well. Marinate in a refrigerator for five to ten minutes.
2. Grind together the ginger, garlic, fresh mint, olive oil, sriracha sauce/red chilli sauce and brown sugar to a smooth mixture.
3. Add the ground mixture to the chicken wings and mix well. Marinate in the refrigerator for eight to ten hours.
4. Preheat the oven to 200°C/400°F/Gas Mark 6.
5. Add one teaspoon onion seeds to the marinated chicken and mix well. Place the wings on a baking tray, spread the marinade over the chicken and sprinkle the remaining onion seeds on top.
6. Place the tray in the preheated oven and bake for twenty minutes.
7. Arrange on a serving plate and serve hot.

Ingredients

8-12 chicken wings
3 tablespoons sriracha sauce (Mexican red chilli sauce/ red chilli sauce)
Salt to taste
2 teaspoons red chilli powder
Juice of ½ lemon
1 inch ginger
8-9 garlic cloves
3-4 fresh mint
2 tablespoons olive oil
1 tablespoon brown sugar
2 teaspoons onion seeds

031

NOODLE CAKES WITH SLICED CHICKEN

Ingredients

200 grams rice noodles
2 boneless chicken breasts, cut into thin slices
1 tablespoon oil + for deep-frying
Salt to taste
1 teaspoon chopped ginger
1 green capsicum, cut into 1-inch pieces
2 teaspoons hoisin sauce
1 fresh red chilli, diagonally sliced

Method

1. Soak the rice noodles in boiling water for five minutes. Drain into another bowl and break into small portions and shape them into rounds
2. Heat sufficient oil in a deep pan. Deep-fry the noodles in the hot oil till crisp. Add a little salt and ginger to the noodles, for a different flavour, before deep-frying.
   Drain onto absorbent paper.
3. Sprinkle the salt on the chicken slices. Drizzle the hoisin sauce and rub in well and marinate for fifteen minutes.
4. Heat one tablespoon oil in a non-stick pan; add the capsicum and salt and cook. Drain the capsicum into a bowl.
5. To the oil remaining in the pan, add the chicken and cook, flip, till evenly cooked on both sides and golden in colour.
6. To serve, place one fried noodle round in a serving plate, place chicken slices over it and top with capsicum. Cover with another noodle round and repeat the process till all the noodle rounds are used up.
7. Sprinkle fresh red chilli slices on top. Serve immediately.

032

DRUMS OF HEAVEN IN CHILLI PLUM SAUCE

Ingredients

8 chicken lollipops
1 teaspoon soy sauce
1 tablespoon garlic paste
3 teaspoons refined flour
1 teaspoon red chilli paste
1 egg
Salt to taste
1 tablespoon sweet chilli sauce
2 teaspoons vinegar
Oil for deep-frying

Sauce

1 teaspoon red chilli paste
8-10 plums, seeded and roughly puréed
2 tablespoons oil
1 medium onion, chopped
1 tablespoon chopped garlic
Salt to taste
1 cup sugar
1 teaspoon vinegar

Method

1. Place the soy sauce, garlic paste, refined flour, red chilli paste, egg and salt in a large bowl and mix well. Add one teaspoon water and mix well. Add the sweet chilli sauce and vinegar and mix. Add the chicken lollipops and mix well.
2. For the sauce, heat two tablespoons oil in a non-stick pan; add the onion and garlic and sauté till they soften. Add the plum purée and mix. Add the salt and red chilli paste and mix well and cook on medium heat. Add the sugar to the sauce and mix till all the sugar dissolves.
3. Add the vinegar and mix well. Remove from the heat and transfer the sauce into a small bowl.
4. Heat sufficient oil in a kadai.
5. Deep-fry the lollipops till cooked and crisp. Drain on absorbent paper.
6. Arrange the lollipops on a serving plate and serve hot with the plum sauce.

033

CHINESE POPCORN PRAWNS

Ingredients

12-16 medium prawns, peeled and deveined
1 egg white
Salt to taste
4 teaspoons cornflour
2 tablespoons oil + for deep-frying
2 inches ginger, finely chopped
10-15 garlic cloves, finely chopped
½ cup tomato ketchup
1 teaspoon grated lemon zest
1 teaspoon crushed red chillies
2 teaspoons vinegar

Method

1. Halve the prawns vertically and place in a bowl. Add the egg white, salt and cornflour, and mix well.
2. Heat sufficient oil in a wok on medium heat.
3. Deep-fry the prawns in hot oil on medium heat till golden in two batches. Drain on absorbent paper.
4. Heat two tablespoons oil in a non-stick pan; add the ginger and garlic and sauté. Add the tomato ketchup and mix well.
5. Add half cup water and mix. Add the lemon zest and crushed red chillies and mix. Add the vinegar and mix.
6. Transfer the prawns into a serving dish, drizzle the sauce over them and serve immediately.

034

CHINESE PRAWN AND MUSHROOM OMLETTE

Ingredients

1 cup small prawns, peeled and deveined
8 button mushrooms, sliced
8 eggs, beaten
1 tablespoon + 4 teaspoons olive oil
2 inches leek stalk, finely sliced
8 teaspoons cornflour
½ cup bean sprouts
1 teaspoon red chilli sauce
2 teaspoons dark soy sauce
Salt to taste

Method

1. For one portion of the filling, heat one-fourth tablespoon olive oil in a non-stick pan. Add one-fourth portion of the leeks and let them sweat for a few seconds. Add one-fourth of the mushrooms and let them sweat for a few seconds.
2. Add two teaspoons cornflour to one-fourth cup prawns and mix well. Add them to the mushrooms and cook on high heat.
3. Add two tablespoons bean sprouts, one-fourth teaspoon red chilli sauce, half teaspoon soy sauce and salt, and mix well.
4. Transfer the mushroom-prawn mixture into a bowl. Set aside.
5. To make one omelette, break two eggs into a bowl, add the salt and whisk well.
6. Heat one teaspoon olive oil in another non-stick pan. Pour the egg mixture and swirl the pan to spread it evenly. Cover and cook till the underside is done and the edges begin to leave the sides of the pan. Remove the cover and flip to cook the other side.

7. Transfer the omelette onto a serving plate; place the mushroom-prawn mixture on one half of the omlette and fold the other half over the mixture.
8. Similarly make three more omlettes with the remaining ingredients. Serve hot.

035

THREE CHILLI PRAWNS

Ingredients

20-24 large prawns, peeled and deveined
½ teaspoon crushed black peppercorns
1 teaspoon red chilli flakes
4 green chillies, finely chopped
2 tablespoons extra virgin olive oil
20-25 garlic cloves, crushed
1 medium onion, roughly chopped
Sea salt to taste
2 teaspoons sugar
1 teaspoon cornflour mixed with 1 tablespoon water

Method

1. Heat the extra virgin olive oil in a non-stick pan. Add the garlic and sauté till brown.
2. Add the onion and sauté for one minute. Add the prawns and sea salt and toss.
3. Add the crushed peppercorns, red chilli flakes, green chillies and sugar and mix well.
4. Add the cornflour mixture to the pan. Mix well and cook till the prawns are done.
5. Serve hot.

036

SHRIMP SPRING ROLLS

Ingredients

8 shrimps, shelled and deveined with tail intact

1 spring onion bulb, finely chopped

8 spring rolls sheets

1 fresh red chilli, finely chopped

1 inch ginger, grated

1 teaspoon sesame oil

Salt to taste

Juice of 1 lemon

1¼ teaspoons cornflour

1 egg, beaten

Oil for deep-frying

Method

1. Place the spring onion in a bowl. Add the fresh red chilli, ginger, sesame oil, salt, shrimps and lemon juice and mix well. Add the cornflour and mix well.
2. Place a spring roll sheet on the worktop. Place a marinated shrimp at one end of the sheet and roll, keeping the tail outside. Seal the ends of the sheets with the beaten egg. Make the remaining spring rolls in the same way.
3. Heat sufficient oil in a wok.
4. Deep-fry the shrimp spring rolls in hot oil till golden. Drain on absorbent paper.
5. Serve hot.

037

SHRIMP AND EGG STIR-FRY

Ingredients

32-36 medium prawns, shelled and deveined

2 eggs, lightly beaten

2 tablespoons oil

3-4 spring onion bulbs, sliced

3-4 garlic cloves, sliced

2 fresh red chillies, chopped

1 teaspoon soy sauce

Salt to taste

2 stalks spring onion greens, cut into ½-inch pieces

Method

1. Heat the oil in a non-stick wok on high heat.
2. Add the spring onions and garlic to the wok and sauté till light brown. Add the prawns and sauté till the prawns are almost done.
3. Add the fresh red chillies, soy sauce and salt and stir.
4. Add the eggs and mix lightly. Add the spring onion greens and mix lightly. Ensure that the eggs do not get dry.
5. Serve hot.

038

HONEY SOY FISH

Ingredients

2 teaspoons honey
1 tablespoon dark soy sauce
1 whole (800 grams) Indian salmon
2-3 fresh red chillies, diagonally sliced
8-10 shallots, sliced
Salt to taste

Garnish

Lemon slices
A few sprigs of fresh coriander, finely chopped
Spring onion green curls

Method

1. Place the fish on a plate; add the soy sauce, honey and red chillies and mix well.
2. Add the shallots and salt, mix and set aside to marinate for ten to fifteen minutes.
3. Preheat oven to 200°C/400°F/Gas Mark 6.
4. Place the marinated fish on a baking tray. Put the baking tray in preheated oven and bake for fifteen to twenty minutes.
5. Garnish with lemon slices, fresh coriander sprigs and spring onion greens curls and serve hot.

Main Course

039

BEAN CURD WITH SOYA GRANULES

Ingredients

300 grams bean curd (tofu), cut into 1-inch pieces

½ cup soya granules

2 teaspoons soy sauce

3 tablespoons sweet red chilli sauce

3 spring onions with greens

1 tablespoon oil

1½ inches ginger, finely chopped

1 tablespoon finely chopped garlic

2 teaspoons cornflour slurry

1 teaspoon vinegar

Method

1. Soak the soya granules in hot water for twenty minutes and drain.
2. Put the bean curd into a bowl. Add one teaspoon soy sauce and one tablespoon chilli sauce and mix well. Set aside for five to ten minutes.
3. Roughly chop the spring onion bulbs and chop the greens. Set aside.
4. Heat the oil in a non-stick pan; add bean curd and sauté well.
5. Add the spring onion bulbs, ginger and garlic, mix well and sauté on high heat.
6. Add the soya granules, mix and cook. Add one-fourth cup water and cook further till the soya granules are done.
7. Add the remaining chilli sauce and remaining soy sauce to the pan and mix well. Add a little water, toss and cook for two minutes.
8. Add the cornflour slurry and vinegar and toss.
9. Add half the spring onion greens and mix well.
10. Serve hot garnished with the remaining spring onion greens.

Image on the opposite page

040

HOT GARLIC PANEER

Ingredients

300 grams cottage cheese, cut into 1-inch cubes

2-3 dried red chillies

1 tablespoon red chilli paste

1 tablespoon red chilli sauce

8-10 garlic cloves, chopped

2 tablespoons oil

2 medium onions, halved, cut into thick slices and layers separated

½ cup Vegetable Stock (page 159)

1 tablespoon soy sauce

Salt to taste

½ teaspoon black pepper powder

3 teaspoons cornflour mixed with ½ cup Vegetable Stock (page 159)

1 medium green capsicum, cut into triangles

1 tablespoon vinegar

Method

1. Heat the oil in a non-stick wok.
2. Break the red chillies into four pieces and remove seeds and add to the wok. Add half the garlic and sauté till fragrant. Add the onions and cottage cheese and toss on high heat.
3. Add one-fourth cup water, red chilli paste and red chilli sauce and toss.
4. Add vegetable stock and mix.
5. Add the soy sauce, salt and pepper powder and mix.
6. Add the cornflour mixture and mix well and cook till sauce thickens.
7. Add the capsicum and remaining garlic and toss again. Cook for a minute longer.
8. Add the vinegar and mix well.
9. Serve hot.

041

CHINESE SIZZLER

Ingredients

For One Portion

50 grams noodles, boiled

4 tablespoons oil + for deep-frying

6-8 spring onions, sliced

5-6 garlic cloves, sliced

Salt to taste

1 teaspoon soy sauce

Black pepper powder to taste

5-6 baby corns, halved

6-8 mushrooms, halved

1 inch ginger

1 medium onion, roughly chopped

50 grams bean curd (tofu), cut into 2 big pieces

6-8 broccoli florets

½ teaspoon crushed red chillies

1 teaspoon cornflour

2 teaspoons honey

1 teaspoon vinegar

½ medium red capsicum, cut into small pieces

3-4 cabbage leaves

Method

1. Heat one tablespoon oil in a non-stick pan. Add half the spring onions and garlic and sauté. Add the noodles, salt, half teaspoon soy sauce, two to three tablespoons water and a pinch of pepper powder and mix. Transfer into a bowl and keep hot.
2. Heat sufficient oil in a deep pan. Add the baby corns to the hot oil and deep-fry for two to three minutes. Add the mushrooms and continue to deep-fry till lightly coloured. Set aside.
3. Place the ginger, remaining spring onions and onion in a chopper and crush.

4. Heat three tablespoons oil in the same non-stick pan in which noodles were cooked; add the crushed mixture and sauté.
5. Add the deep-fried baby corns and the mushrooms to the pan. Add the salt, half teaspoon pepper powder and mix well and transfer into another bowl.
6. Add the tofu to the oil remaining in the pan and shallow-fry, flip, and cook till golden on all sides. Drain on absorbent paper and transfer to a plate.
7. Add the broccoli florets to the pan; add half cup water, salt, crushed red chillies and cook.
8. Add half teaspoon soy sauce to the pan and mix. Add the cornflour mixed in two tablespoons water and mix.
9. Add the honey and vinegar and mix well. Transfer the broccoli florets to a plate.
10. In the sauce remaining in the pan, add red capsicum and mix well.
11. Heat the sizzler plate.
12. Place the hot sizzler plate on its wooden base. Line the iron plate with cabbage leaves. Spread the noodles in the centre, place the deep-fried vegetables on one side of the noodles and place the bean curd over them. Place the broccoli florets on the other side of the noodles. Place the red capsicum over the bean curd pieces and serve immediately.

042

FRESH ALMONDS IN SPICY ORANGE SAUCE

Ingredients

½ cup peeled fresh almonds

1 cup orange juice

2 tablespoons oil

1 teaspoon chopped ginger

1 medium onion, diced

½ cup blanched and peeled almonds

8-10 broccoli florets

Salt to taste

1 teaspoon red chilli sauce

1 tablespoon cornflour

½ green capsicum, chopped

A pinch of finely chopped dried red chillies

Method

1. Heat the oil in a non-stick pan, add the ginger, onion, fresh almonds, blanched almonds, broccoli, orange juice, salt and chilli sauce and sauté.
2. Mix the cornflour with a quarter cup water.
3. Add the green capsicum and the cornflour mixture and mix well.
4. Add the dried red chillies and mix well.
5. Transfer into a serving bowl and serve hot with hot steamed rice.

043

HOT AND SPICY ASIAN VEGETABLES WITH SUNFLOWER SEEDS

Ingredients

2 fresh red chillies, diagonally sliced

¼ small cabbage, roughly chopped

½ medium broccoli, separated into small florets and blanched

4 pak choi

1 tablespoon black sunflower seeds

2 tablespoons oil

3-4 spring onions, chopped

2 inches ginger, grated

10 garlic cloves, chopped

Salt to taste

½ teaspoon black pepper powder

1 teaspoon soy sauce

1 teaspoon cornflour

Method

1. Dry-roast the sunflower seeds for a couple of minutes, on medium heat, and transfer into a bowl. Set aside.
2. Heat the oil in a non-stick pan; add the spring onions and sauté. Add the cabbage and mix.
3. Add the ginger and garlic and continue to sauté. Add half cup water and cook.
4. Tear the pak choi and add along with broccoli florets, salt, pepper powder and soy sauce and mix well.
5. Add the fresh red chillies and mix. Mix the cornflour with a quarter cup water and add to the pan, a little at time, and mix. Cook till the sauce thickens a little.
6. Transfer into a serving bowl, sprinkle the sunflower seeds and serve hot.

044

STIR-FRIED BEAN CURD WITH LEMONGRASS AND CHILLIES

Ingredients

675 grams firm bean curd (tofu), cut into 1-inch cubes

2 one inch lemongrass stalks, bruised and chopped

2 fresh red chillies, seeded and chopped

12 dried shiitake mushrooms, trimmed

2 tablespoons oil + for deep-frying

4 tablespoons hoisin sauce

2 tablespoons soy sauce

1½ tablespoons tomato purée

2 leeks (white part only), sliced

1 large red capsicum, cut into 1-inch squares

1 large green capsicum, cut into 1-inch squares

½ teaspoon black pepper powder

Method

1. Soak the shiitake mushrooms in one cup of boiling water for half an hour. Drain and reserve the soaking liquid.
2. Place the bean curd cubes between double layers of paper towel and press gently so that all the extra moisture is absorbed.
3. Heat sufficient oil in a wok and deep-fry the bean curd cubes, a few at a time, over medium heat till golden brown. Drain on absorbent paper.
4. Mix together the reserved soaking liquid, hoisin sauce, soy sauce, tomato purée and red chillies in a bowl.
5. Heat two tablespoons oil in another wok. Add the leeks and lemongrass and stir-fry over medium heat for about one minute or till tender. Add the red and green capsicums and mushrooms and stir-fry for one minute longer.

6. Stir in the sauce mixture and fried bean curd cubes and bring the mixture to a boil. Cook over medium heat, stirring frequently, for about two minutes or till the sauce thickens slightly.
7. Transfer into a serving dish, sprinkle the pepper powder and serve immediately.

045

GREEN BEANS STIR-FRY

Ingredients

- 12-15 French beans, cut into 1-inch pieces
- 2 tablespoons sesame oil
- 5-6 button mushrooms sliced
- 1 medium carrot, sliced and halved
- ¼ cup canned water chestnuts, halved
- 2 tablespoons black bean sauce
- 1 teaspoon crushed red chillies
- 2 teaspoons red chilli sauce
- Salt to taste
- Toasted white sesame seeds, for garnishing
- Fresh coriander, for garnishing

Method

1. Heat the sesame oil in a non-stick wok. Add the French beans, mushrooms and carrot. Toss on high heat. Sprinkle a little water.
2. Add the water chestnuts and mix well. Add the black bean sauce and crushed red chillies. Toss again and cook for three to four minutes.
3. Add the chilli sauce and salt. Mix well and cook for one minute.
4. Serve hot garnished with the toasted white sesame seeds and fresh coriander.

046

KUNG PAO POTATOES

Ingredients

4 large potatoes, boiled, peeled and cubed
¼ cup roasted peanuts
4 tablespoons oil
2 tablespoons chilli oil
3-4 dried red chillies, broken
6 spring onions, sliced
1 inch ginger, finely chopped
4-5 garlic cloves, finely chopped
2 tablespoons soy sauce
1 tablespoon red chilli sauce
2 teaspoons sugar
Salt to taste
¾ cup Vegetable Stock (page 159)
2 teaspoons cornflour, mixed in ¼ cup Vegetable Stock (page 159)
2 stalks spring onion greens, chopped

Method

1. Heat the oil in a non-stick pan. Add the potato cubes and shallow-fry till light golden. Drain on absorbent paper.
2. Heat the chilli oil in another non-stick pan. Add the red chillies and sauté for half minute or till crisp. Add the spring onions, ginger and garlic and sauté till soft.
3. Add the soy sauce, red chilli sauce, sugar, salt and peanuts and mix. Add the vegetable stock and mix well.
4. Add the cornflour mixture to the pan and cook till the sauce thickens.
5. Add the potatoes and mix gently. Serve immediately garnished with the spring onion greens.

047

LONG BEANS WITH HONEY SESAME

Ingredients

250 grams long beans

4 tablespoons honey

2 tablespoons toasted sesame seeds

3 tablespoons oil

7-8 garlic cloves, chopped

2 inches ginger, chopped

1 tablespoon dark soy sauce

2 tablespoons red chilli paste

Salt to taste

2 tablespoons crushed toasted peanuts

Method

1. Trim the two ends of the beans and blanch them in boiling water for two minutes. Drain.
2. Heat the oil in a non-stick wok. Add the garlic and ginger and sauté. Add the dark soy sauce, red chilli paste, one-fourth cup water and salt and mix well.
3. Add the beans and mix. Add the honey and mix. Add the peanuts and mix.
4. Transfer the beans into a serving plate, drizzle the sauce remaining in the wok over them, garnish with the sesame seeds and serve hot.

048

MIXED VEGETABLE MANCHURIAN

Ingredients

1 medium cabbage, grated

1 medium carrot, grated

8-10 French beans, finely chopped

1 medium green capsicum, finely chopped

2-3 garlic cloves, finely chopped

½ inch ginger, finely chopped

2 green chillies, finely chopped

Salt to taste

½ cup refined flour

Oil for deep-frying

Mixed capsicum curls for garnishing

Thin strip of spring onion green, tied into a knot

Sauce

2 tablespoons oil

1 medium onion, finely chopped

2 inches celery stalk, finely chopped

1 inch ginger, finely chopped

4-6 garlic cloves, finely chopped

3 green chillies, finely chopped

2 tablespoons light soy sauce

2 cups Vegetable Stock (page 159)

3 medium spring onion greens, finely chopped

Salt to taste

1 teaspoon sugar

3 tablespoons cornflour, mixed with ½ cup water

1 tablespoon white vinegar

Method

1. Place the cabbage, carrot, beans, capsicum, garlic, ginger, green chillies and salt in a bowl and mix with hand mashing them slightly. Add the refined flour and mix.

2. Heat sufficient oil in a wok. Shape the vegetable mixture into small balls and gently slide them into the hot oil and deep-fry till golden. Drain on absorbent paper.
3. For the sauce, heat two tablespoons oil in a non-stick wok. Add the onion, celery, ginger, garlic and green chillies and sauté. Add the soy sauce and vegetable stock and mix.
4. Add the spring onion greens, salt and sugar to the sauce and mix. Add the cornflour mixture and mix. Add the vinegar and mix. Cook till the sauce thickens slightly.
5. Add the fried vegetable balls and mixed lightly.
6. Serve hot garnished with capsicum curls and a spring onion green strip tied into a knot.

049

PINEAPPLE PEPPER STIR-FRY

Ingredients

10 pineapple slices, cut into 1-inch pieces

1 large red capsicum, cut into triangles

1 large yellow capsicum, cut into triangles

1 large green capsicum, cut into triangles

3 tablespoons oil

Salt to taste

4 tablespoons red chilli sauce

1 teaspoon crushed red chillies

2 tablespoons honey

1 tablespoon lemon juice

Method

1. Heat the oil in a non-stick pan; add the capsicums and salt and sauté for five minutes.
2. Add the pineapple, red chillli sauce, crushed red chillies and honey and mix.
3. Add the lemon juice and mix.
4. Serve hot.

050

SICHUAN-STYLE EGGPLANT

Ingredients

500 grams long brinjals
2 tablespoons hot black bean sauce
Salt to taste
3 tablespoons dark soy sauce
4 tablespoons cornflour
2 tablespoons oil + for deep-frying
2 spring onions, cut into four pieces
1 inch ginger, chopped
2 fresh red chillies, cut into long slices
8-10 Sichuan peppers, crushed
7-8 black peppercorns, crushed
1½ cups Vegetable Stock (page 159)
2 tablespoons malt vinegar
1 teaspoon sugar

Method

1. Heat sufficient oil in a kadai. Gently slide in the eggplant cubes into hot oil and deep-fry till light brown. Drain on absorbent paper. Set aside.
2. Deep-fry red capsicum in the same hot oil till they become bright in color. Drain on absorbent paper. Set aside.
3. Deep-fry the fresh basil in the same hot oil till crisp. Drain on absorbent paper. Set aside.
4. Grind the dried red chillies to a fine paste.
5. Heat two tablespoons oil in a non-stick wok; add the garlic and onion and sauté till the garlic is light brown. Add the ground chilli paste, hoisin sauce and soy sauce and mix well. Add fried eggplants and vegetable stock and mix well.
6. Add the spring onion with greens to the wok and mix well.
7. Add the cornflour slurry and cook till the mixture thickens. Add the fried capsicum and mix well.
8. Add chilli vinegar and continue to cook for three to four minutes.
9. Transfer the eggplant curry into a serving platter, garnish with fried basil and serve hot.

051

SWEET AND SOUR FRUIT AND VEGETABLES

Ingredients

2 slices of tinned pineapple, each slice quartered

8-10 lychees

¾ medium red capsicum, cut into ½-inch pieces

¼ medium green capsicum, cut into ½-inch pieces

10-15 broccoli florets

1 tablespoon oil

3 spring onion bulbs, halved

1 cup Vegetable Stock (page 159)

2 tablespoons tomato ketchup

Salt to taste

2 teaspoons cornflour

2 teaspoons sugar

2 teaspoons vinegar

Method

1. Heat the oil in a non-stick wok. Add the spring onions and sauté.
2. Add the capsicums, broccoli florets and vegetable stock and mix. Add the pineapple and lychees and mix.
3. Add the tomato ketchup and mix well. Add the salt and mix well.
4. Mix the cornflour with one-fourth cup water and add one tablespoon of this mixture to the wok and mix. Cook till the sauce thickens.
5. Add the sugar and vinegar and mix well.
6. Transfer into a serving bowl and serve hot.

Ingredients

1 lotus root, cut into 1-inch thick diagonal slices

1 teaspoon freshly crushed black peppercorns

Salt to taste

3 tablespoons cornflour

2 tablespoon olive oil + for deep-frying

½ inch ginger, sliced

1 inch celery stalk, chopped

1-2 fresh red chillies, diagonally sliced

2-3 garlic cloves, roughly chopped

1 medium carrot, cut diagonally into

4 pieces and blanched

8-10 French beans, cut into 3-inch pieces and blanched

10-12 snow peas, stringed, cut diagonally into 2 pieces and blanched

Fresh coriander sprigs, for garnishing

052

STIR-FRIED LOTUS ROOT WITH BLACK PEPPER

Method

1. Place lotus root in a bowl. Add the salt and two tablespoons cornflour and rub well into the lotus root.
2. Heat sufficient oil in a wok. Add the lotus root and deep-fry till golden brown and crisp. Drain on absorbent paper and set aside.
3. Heat two tablespoons oil in a non-stick wok; add the ginger, celery and garlic and red chillies and toss. Add the carrots and beans and toss. Add half cup water and let the beans cook. Add the snow peas and mix. Cook for a minute.
4. Add the lotus root and toss.
5. Add the remaining cornflour mixed in one tablespoon water and cook till the mixture is slightly thick. Add the crushed peppercorns and salt and mix.
6. Serve hot, garnished with fresh coriander sprigs.

053

THREE TREASURE VEGETABLES

Ingredients

2 medium carrots, cut into diamonds

3-4 spring onion bulbs, quartered

150 grams bean curd (tofu), cut into 1-inch triangles

1 medium broccoli, separated into medium florets

2 tablespoons oil

2 teaspoons garlic paste

1½ cups Vegetable Stock (page 159)

Salt to taste

1 teaspoon sugar

10 almonds, blanched and peeled

¼ teaspoon crushed red chillies

2½ teaspoons cornflour, mixed in ¼ cup water

1 tablespoon vinegar

Spring onion greens, for garnishing

Method

1. Heat the oil in a non-stick wok. Add the garlic paste and sauté for a few seconds. Add the spring onions and carrots and continue to sauté.
2. Add one cup vegetable stock, salt and sugar and mix. Add the bean curd, broccoli, almonds and mix. Add half cup vegetable stock and mix.
3. Add the crushed red chillies and cornflour mixture. Mix well and cook till the sauce thickens.
4. Add the vinegar, mix and take the wok off the heat.
5. Serve hot immediately, garnished with spring onion greens.

054

YIN YAN BEAN CURD

Ingredients

100 grams silken bean curd (tofu)
100 grams firm bean curd (tofu)
2 teaspoons cornflour
Salt to taste
1 spring onion bulb, sliced

Yin sauce

1 cup Vegetable Stock (page 159)
1 teaspoon oyster sauce

Yan sauce

2 tablespoons oil
1 tablespoon chopped garlic
5 tablespoons tomato ketchup
2 teaspoons red chilli sauce
1 spring onion green, sliced

Method

1. For the Yan sauce bean curd, heat two tablespoons oil in a non-stick wok.
2. Add garlic and sauté till lightly browned. Add four tablespoons tomato ketchup, red chilli sauce and mix. Add firm bean curd cubes and mix.
3. Mix cornflour with two tablespoons water and add one tablespoon of this mixture to the wok and cook till the sauce thickens. Add the remaining tomato ketchup and salt and mix.
4. For the Yin sauce bean curd, heat one cup vegetable stock in another non-stick wok. Add oyster sauce and mix well.
5. Add the silken bean curd to the pan and mix. Add the remaining cornflour mixture and mix. Add salt to taste and mix gently.
6. Transfer the two bean curd mixtures into two separate compartments of a yin yan serving bowl. Add the spring onion bulbs to the silken bean curd and the spring onion greens to firm bean curd. Serve hot.

055

STIR-FRIED VEGETABLES WITH FRIED BASIL

Ingredients

4-5 baby corns, diagonally sliced

1 medium cucumber, peeled, halved, seeded and cut into thick slices

10-12 shiitake mushrooms, soaked (optional)

1 medium red capsicum, sliced thickly

½ cup fresh basil

1 tablespoon oil + for deep-frying

1 medium onion, sliced

3 garlic cloves, sliced

7-8 water chestnuts, sliced

10-12 cashew nuts

1 teaspoon brown sugar

Salt to taste

1 teaspoon soy sauce

1 teaspoon rice vinegar

Method

1. Heat one tablespoon oil in a non-stick wok.
2. Add the onion, garlic and baby corns and mix. Stir-fry for two minutes.
3. Add the water chestnuts, cucumber, cashew nuts, shiitake mushrooms, brown sugar, salt and red capsicum and toss.
4. Add the soy sauce and mix, cook for two to three minutes.
5. Add the rice vinegar and mix well.
6. Transfer the vegetables onto a serving plate.
7. Heat sufficient oil in a wok. Add the fresh basil and deep-fry till crisp.
8. Drain on absorbent paper and garnish the vegetables.
9. Serve hot with steamed rice.

056

STIR-FRIED EGGPLANT WITH BEANS

Ingredients

2 long brinjal, cut into round slices

10-12 French beans, stringed and cut into 2-inch pieces

1 tablespoon oil

1 medium onion, halved and sliced

Salt to taste

1 tablespoon soy sauce

1 tablespoon finely chopped garlic

4 green chillies, sliced diagonally

250 grams silken bean curd (tofu), cut into fingers

½ teaspoon sugar

1 tablespoon cornflour, mixed in ¼ cup water

1 teaspoon vinegar

Diagonally sliced fresh red chilli, for garnishing

A fresh coriander sprig, for garnishing

Method

1. Heat the oil in a non-stick wok. Add the onion, brinjal, salt and soy sauce and cook on high heat for two minutes.
2. Add the beans and garlic, mix and cook on high heat for three to four minutes.
3. Add the green chillies and mix. Cook for two minutes.
4. Add the bean curd, sugar, cornflour slurry and vinegar. Mix and cook for one minute.
5. Transfer into a serving bowl and serve hot garnished with fresh red chilli and a coriander sprig.

057

STIR-FRIED BEAN CURD WITH ASIAN GREENS

Ingredients

- 200 grams silken bean curd (tofu), cut into ¾-inch cubes
- ½ medium broccoli, separated into medium florets
- ½ medium cabbage, shredded
- 4 pak choi, torn
- 2 teaspoons oil
- 2 inches ginger, grated
- Salt to taste
- ½ teaspoon black pepper powder
- 1 tablespoon lemon juice
- 10 garlic cloves, chopped
- 1 tablespoon soy sauce

Method

1. Keep the broccoli florets in a bowl of water.
2. Heat one teaspoon oil in a non-stick pan; add the bean curd and ginger and mix. Add the salt and half the pepper powder. Cook for a few minutes tossing the bean curd so that they get cooked evenly from all sides. Remove from heat and add lemon juice. Mix well and set aside.
3. Heat the remaining oil in another non-stick pan. Add the garlic and sauté for a minute. Drain the broccoli and add along with the cabbage and pak choi and mix.
4. Toss the greens and add a little water. Toss again and add the salt and remaining pepper powder. Add the soy sauce and toss again. Cook the greens for three to four minutes.
5. Toss the greens once more and transfer to a serving dish and spread. Place the bean curd over the greens and serve hot.

058

TOMATO AND EGG CHINESE-STYLE

Ingredients

5-6 medium tomatoes, cut each into 8 pieces

4 eggs

2 tablespoons oil

3 spring onion bulbs, sliced

2 green chillies, roughly sliced

½ teaspoon soy sauce

1 tablespoon sweet red chilli sauce

Salt to taste

8-10 fresh coriander sprigs, finely chopped

4 teaspoons cornflour slurry

Method

1. Heat the oil in a non-stick pan. Add the tomatoes and sauté for two to three minutes and drain on an absorbent paper and transfer to a bowl.
2. Add the spring onion bulbs to the same pan and sauté lightly.
3. Break the eggs into a bowl, beat them lightly and add to the pan.
4. Add the green chillies and cook on high heat till the eggs are scrambled.
5. Add the soy sauce and chilli sauce and mix well. Add the tomatoes and salt and toss. Sprinkle a little water and cook.
6. Add chopped coriander and cornflour slurry, mix well and cook for a minute.
7. Serve hot.

059

CHINESE CHICKEN

Ingredients

200 grams boneless chicken, cut into small pieces
2 tablespoons oil
5 spring onions, roughly chopped
2 teaspoons soy sauce
1 tablespoon oyster sauce
1 tablespoon Sichuan sauce
1 teaspoon sugar
1 teaspoon vinegar
2 stalks spring onion greens, chopped
2 teaspoons toasted sesame seeds
½ cup crushed fried noodles

Method

1. Heat the oil in a non-stick wok; add the spring onions, chicken and soy sauce and mix.
2. Add the oyster sauce and mix well. Add the Sichuan sauce and mix. Add the sugar and vinegar; mix well and cook till the chicken is done.
3. Put the spring onion greens in a bowl.
4. Place the chicken on the spring onion greens. Add one teaspoon toasted sesame seeds and crushed fried noodles and mix.
5. Transfer into a serving dish, sprinkle the remaining toasted sesame seeds and serve hot.

060

CHENGFU CHICKEN

Ingredients

300 grams boneless chicken breasts, cut into1-inch pieces

2 tablespoons cornflour

2 teaspoons dark soy sauce

4 tablespoons oil + for deep-frying

20-25 garlic cloves, peeled

8-10 fresh spinach leaves, torn

Salt to taste

15-20 spring onion bulbs, roughly chopped

2 tablespoons oyster sauce

1 teaspoon crushed red chillies

1 tablespoon white vinegar

8-10 Sichuan peppers

Method

1. Place the chicken in a glass bowl; add the cornflour and dark soy sauce and mix. Set aside.
2. Heat two tablespoons oil in a non-stick pan.
3. Add the garlic cloves to the pan and sauté, on medium heat, till well browned.
4. Add the spinach leaves and a little salt and sauté for a while. Transfer into a serving bowl and set aside.
5. Heat sufficient oil in a wok and deep-fry the chicken on high heat till golden brown. Drain on absorbent paper.
6. Heat two tablespoons oil in the same non-stick pan; add the spring onions and sauté. Add the chicken and mix. Add the oyster sauce, salt, crushed red chillies and vinegar and toss.
7. Crush the Sichuan peppers and add to the pan and mix well.
8. Transfer into the serving bowl over the garlic-spinach mixture and serve hot.

061

SICHUAN SPICED CHICKEN

Ingredients

400 grams boneless chicken, sliced
A pinch of crushed Sichuan peppers
20 dried red chillies, boiled
14-16 dried round red chillies
3 teaspoons ginger paste
3 teaspoons garlic paste
1 teaspoon soy sauce
Salt to taste
3 tablespoons oil
1 medium onion, chopped
1 tablespoon chopped garlic
2 tablespoons tomato ketchup
1 tablespoon vinegar
Spring onion greens, for garnishing

Method

1. Grind the boiled red chillies to a fine paste. Set aside.
2. Mix together the ginger paste, garlic paste, soy sauce, one tablespoon red chilli paste in a bowl. Add the chicken and salt and mix well and marinate for one hour.
3. Heat the oil in a non-stick wok; add the round chillies and onion and sauté till the onion turns a light brown.
4. Add chopped garlic and sauté for one minute. Add the chicken with the marinade and mix well and cook till chicken is almost done.
5. Add the tomato ketchup and mix well. Add a pinch of crushed Sichuan peppers, salt and vinegar and mix well.
6. Transfer into a serving bowl, garnish with spring onion greens and serve hot.

062

FIERY SICHUAN CHICKEN

Ingredients

400 grams boneless chicken, cut into ¾-inch pieces

1 tablespoon Sichuan peppercorns, roasted and crushed

6 dried red chillies, chopped

1 tablespoon red chilli sauce

4 tablespoons oil

½ small green cabbage, shredded

½ small red cabbage, shredded

Salt to taste

10-15 garlic cloves, crushed

2 tablespoons oyster sauce

1 tablespoon dark soy sauce

2 teaspoons cornflour

1 teaspoon sesame oil

Chopped spring onion greens, for garnishing

Method

1. Heat a non-stick pan and pour two tablespoons oil. Add both the cabbages to the pan and add salt and cook till done. Transfer the cabbage into a serving dish. Keep warm.
2. Heat another non-stick pan and pour two tablespoons oil. Add garlic and sauté till brown. Add red chillies and continue to sauté.
3. Add chicken and mix well and continue to sauté. Add Sichuan peppercorns, red chilli sauce, oyster sauce and dark soy sauce and mix. Cook till the chicken is done.
4. Add the cornflour mixed with half cup water and salt to the chicken and mix well. Cook till the sauce thickens.
5. Arrange the chicken over the cabbage. Drizzle the sesame oil and garnish with spring onion greens. Serve hot with steamed rice.

063

STIR-FRIED CHICKEN WITH BASIL AND CHILLI

Ingredients

4 boneless chicken breasts, cut into strips

1 cup fresh basil

6-8 fresh red chillies, diagonally sliced

1 tablespoon fish sauce

2 tablespoons oil + for deep-frying

2 tablespoons chopped garlic

1 tablespoon soy sauce

Salt to taste

1 teaspoon sugar

Method

1. Place the chicken in a bowl; add fish sauce and mix. Set aside.
2. Heat two tablespoons oil in a non-stick wok; add the garlic and sauté on high heat till lightly browned.
3. Add the chicken mixed with the fish sauce to the wok and stir.
4. Add the red chillies and soy sauce to chicken and mix well. Add the salt and sugar and stir. Cook till the chicken is done.
5. Heat sufficient oil in another wok. Squeeze out excess water from basil and add to the hot oil and deep-fry till crisp. Strain the basil through a sieve.
6. Add fried basil to the chicken and toss. Serve hot.

064

STEAMED TOFU WITH MINCED CHICKEN

Ingredients

75 grams bean curd (tofu), cut into ½-inch cubes

100 grams minced chicken

Salt to taste

1 teaspoon soy sauce

1½ teaspoons cornflour

1 egg

2 banana leaves

1 small broccoli, separated into small florets

4 teaspoons sesame oil

Black pepper powder to taste

Garnish

Black and white sesame seeds, for sprinkling

A few fresh coriander springs

Red chilli oil, for drizzling

Method

1. Place the minced chicken in a bowl; add the salt, soy sauce, cornflour and egg and mix well.
2. Boil one and a half cups water in a wide non-stick pan. Line a bamboo steamer with banana leaves. Place a ring mould that will fit in the steamer.
3. Place minced chicken mixture in it and top it with tofu.
4. Arrange the broccoli florets over the tofu; drizzle the sesame oil and sprinkle salt and pepper powder.
5. Place the bamboo steamer in the boiling water pan; cover with the bamboo lid and steam for ten minutes.
6. Remove the lid and garnish with the black and white sesame seeds and fresh coriander sprig and drizzle red chilli oil over the chicken. Serve hot.

065

STIR-FRIED SIZZLING CHICKEN

Method

1. Grind the garlic, ginger, green chilli and fresh coriander with a little amount of water to a coarse paste. Set aside.
2. Heat half tablespoon oil in a non-stick pan.
3. Add the spring onion bulb, carrot and French beans to the pan and sauté lightly. Set aside.
4. Add the coarse paste mixed with one-fourth cup water. Cook for one to two minutes.
5. Add the sugar and cornflour mixture and mix. Cook till the sauce thickens. Add the vinegar, mix and adjust the salt. Set aside.
6. Place chicken in a bowl; add the salt and pepper powder and mix.
7. Heat the remaining oil in a non-stick grill pan and grill the chicken, turn over and cook till both sides are golden. Remove from heat and slice thickly. Set aside.
8. Heat the sizzler plate.
9. Keep the hot sizzler plate over its wooden base. Line the hot sizzler platter with red cabbage leaves, place the tossed vegetables and chicken slices over it.
10. Drizzle the vegetable sauce and chilli oil and serve immediately with rice or noodles.

Ingredients

For One Portion

- 100 grams boneless skinless chicken breasts
- ½ garlic clove, roughly chopped
- ¼ inch ginger, roughly chopped
- ½ green chilli, roughly chopped
- ⅓ cup fresh coriander leaves
- 1 tablespoon oil
- 1 spring onion bulb, sliced
- ¼ medium carrot, cut into round slices
- 2 French beans, cut into 1-inch pieces
- Salt to taste
- A pinch of black pepper powder
- ¼ teaspoon sugar
- ½ teaspoon cornflour, mixed with ½ tablespoon water
- ½ teaspoon vinegar
- Red cabbage leaves as required
- ¼ teaspoon chilli oil

066

STIR-FRIED CHICKEN WITH EGGPLANT

Ingredients

2 boneless chicken breasts, cut into 1-inch cubes
2 medium brinjals, cut into thin round slices
1 tablespoon oil
Salt to taste
1 medium onion, sliced
2 tablespoons crushed garlic
1 teaspoon dark soy sauce
1 tablespoon red chilli paste
1 tablespoon tomato ketchup
Crushed black peppercorns to taste
1 teaspoon vinegar
Sesame oil, for drizzling
1 stalk spring onion greens, cut into ½ inch diagonal pieces

Method

1. Heat the oil in a non-stick pan. Add the brinjal and salt and sauté till lightly browned.
2. Add the onion and mix well. Add the garlic and mix well.
3. Add the chicken and mix well. Add the dark soy sauce, red chilli paste and tomato ketchup and mix well. Add the crushed peppercorns and cook till the chicken is done. Add the vinegar and mix well.
4. Transfer into a serving plate, drizzle sesame oil, garnish with spring onion greens and serve hot.

067

GREEN CHICKEN STIR-FRY

Ingredients

400 grams boneless chicken breasts, sliced thinly

2 tablespoons oil

10-12 garlic cloves, crushed

8 spring onion bulbs, sliced

10-12 French beans, halved vertically and cut into 1-inch pieces

¼ medium green capsicum, chopped

Salt to taste

Black pepper powder to taste

2 teaspoons soy sauce

4 pak choi

20-25 roasted cashew nuts

10-15 fresh basil

1 tablespoon cornflour

3 fresh red chillies, sliced diagonally

Method

1. Heat the oil in a non-stick wok; add the garlic and spring onions and sauté.
2. Add the French beans, chicken, capsicum, salt, pepper powder and soy sauce and stir.
3. Tear the pak choi and add to the wok. Toss well.
4. Add the cashew nuts, a little water and fresh basil and mix well.
5. Mix cornflour with three tablespoons water. Add the cornflour mixture along with fresh red chillies. Cook till chicken is done and the mixture thick.
6. Serve hot with steaming hot noodles or rice.

068

SWEET SOY CHICKEN

Ingredients

4 boneless chicken breasts
1½ tablespoons brown sugar
1 tablespoon honey
¼ cup + 2 teaspoons dark soy sauce
1½ inches ginger, grated
Salt to taste
1 tablespoon olive oil
2 cups cooked white rice
½ cup Chicken Stock (page 159)
8 teaspoons butter
2 teaspoons red chilli flakes
1 tablespoon sesame seeds

Method

1. Mix one-fourth cup dark soy sauce and brown sugar in a bowl. Add the ginger and mix well.
2. Sprinkle a little salt over the chicken breasts. Dip them, one by one, in the soy mixture and put into a zip lock bag. Pour the remaining marinade also into the bag and seal the bag. Keep it in a refrigerator to marinate for three to four hours.
3. Heat the olive oil in a non-stick pan; add the chicken breasts and cook on medium heat, turning sides so that they get cooked evenly from all sides. Add the remaining soy sauce to the chicken in the pan and cook till the chicken is done.
4. Drizzle the honey over the chicken and mix. Place the chicken on a chopping board and make a few slits on each breast.
5. Place the rice in a microwave-safe bowl; add the chicken stock, salt, butter and red chilli flakes and cook in the microwave oven.
6. Take the rice out of the microwave oven. Place a ring mould on a serving plate, pack some of the rice into it and press lightly. Similarly use up the remaining rice. Remove the ring mould gently. Place the chicken on the rice, drizzle the sauce remaining in the pan over them, sprinkle the sesame seeds and serve hot.

069

HONEY WALNUT PRAWNS

Ingredients

16 prawns, shelled and deveined
3 tablespoons honey
8-10 walnut kernels
4-5 tablespoons oil
Salt to taste
1¼ teaspoons crushed red chillies
2 teaspoons + 1 tablespoon lemon juice
3½ teaspoons soy sauce
2 tablespoons cornflour
7-8 garlic cloves, crushed
12-15 dried button red chillies
¼ small green capsicum, cut into small cubes
¼ small yellow capsicum, cut into small cubes
¼ small red capsicum, cut into small cubes

Method

1. Heat the oil in non-stick wok.
2. Place the prawns in a bowl; add the salt, one-fourth teaspoon crushed red chillies, two teaspoons lemon juice, one and a half teaspoons soy sauce and cornflour and mix well.
3. Put the prawns in the wok and sauté on high heat till golden. Drain on absorbent paper and set aside.
4. Keeping one tablespoon oil, remove excess oil from the wok into a bowl. Add the garlic and red chillies to the wok and sauté for one minute.
5. Add the walnut kernels, capsicums, salt, remaining crushed red chillies and toss.
6. Add very little water and the remaining soy sauce. Toss again.
7. Add the fried prawns, one tablespoon lemon juice and honey. Toss and cook for one minute.
8. Serve hot.

Ingredients

250 grams boneless chicken, thinly sliced

10-12 baby corn, sliced diagonally

3 tablespoons oyster sauce

2 tablespoons cornflour

1 cup + 3 tablespoons Chicken Stock (page 159)

2 tablespoons oil

2 large garlic cloves, sliced

1 medium onion, quartered and layers separated

1 tablespoon dark soy sauce

Salt to taste

½ teaspoons crushed black peppercorns

2 stalks spring onion greens, sliced diagonally

3-4 fresh basil leaves + 1 sprig for garnishing

Red capsicum strips for garnishing

070

SLICED CHICKEN WITH BABY CORN IN OYSTER SAUCE

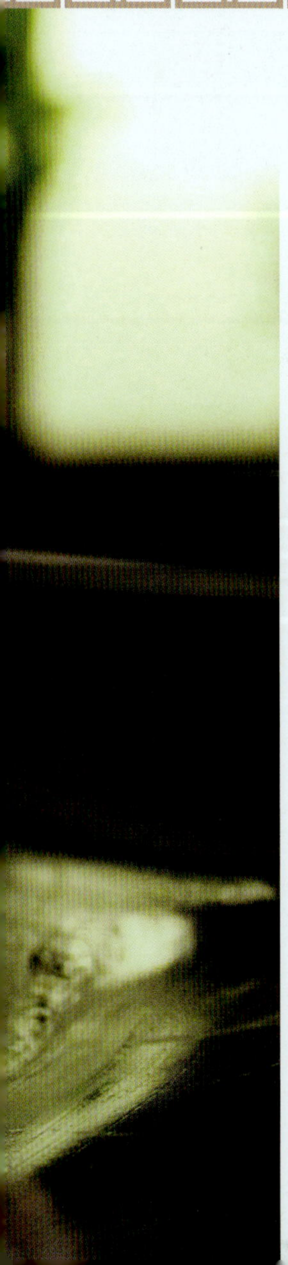

Method

1. Mix cornflour with three tablespoons chicken stock to make a slurry and set aside.
2. Heat oil in a non-stick wok, add garlic and onion and sauté till they become light golden brown.
3. Add chicken and stir-fry for a few minutes. Add baby corn and toss for a minute.
4. Add oyster sauce, soy sauce, remaining chicken stock, salt and crushed peppercorns and bring to a boil.
5. Add cornflour slurry and cook, stirring continuously, till the sauce thickens.
6. Add spring onion greens and basil leaves and mix. Remove from heat and transfer into a serving bowl.
7. Garnish with red capsicum strips and basil sprig, serve hot with steamed rice.

071

CREAMY PRAWNS

Ingredients

12-15 medium prawns, shelled and deveined with tail intact

3 eggs

Salt to taste

2-3 tablespoons milk

3 tablespoons oil

½ medium green capsicum, finely chopped

½ medium red capsicum, finely chopped

1 tablespoon red chilli sauce

2 teaspoons cornflour slurry

2 cups cooked rice

Method

1. Break the eggs into a bowl; add the salt and whisk well. Add the milk and whisk again. Set aside.
2. Heat one tablespoon oil in a non-stick pan; add the green capsicum, red capsicum and salt and mix well. Set aside.
3. Place the prawns in a bowl; add the red chilli sauce and mix well.
4. Heat one tablespoon oil in a non-stick wok; add the prawns and glaze. Transfer the prawns into a bowl and rest for two to three minutes.
5. Heat the remaining oil in the same non-stick wok; add half the egg-milk mixture and stir. Remove from heat and keep stirring. Add the remaining egg-milk mixture and stir. Add the prawns and mix well. Add the cornflour slurry and cook till the mixture thickens and prawns are done.
6. Spread the cooked rice on a serving platter, top with the creamy prawns and sautéed capsicums and serve immediately.

072

CHILLI FISH WITH CRUSHED POTATOES

Ingredients

400 gram boneless basa fish fillets, cut into 1-inch cubes

2 tablespoons chilli oil

5-6 medium potatoes, boiled and peeled

2 tablespoons olive oil

10-15 cherry tomatoes, halved

10-15 green olives, pitted

10-15 black olives, pitted

Sea salt to taste

2 brown bread slices

A little fresh parsley

3-4 tablespoons extra virgin olive oil

Crushed black peppercorns to taste

2 teaspoons lemon juice

Method

1. Heat the olive oil in a non-stick pan; add the cherry tomatoes, green olives and black olives and mix. Add the sea salt to the pan. Mash the potatoes and add. Mix well.
2. Tear the bread slices and put into a mixer jar, add the parsley and crush to get a coarse mixture. Add the crushed bread-parsley mixture, extra virgin olive oil, salt and pepper to the potatoes and mix well. Set aside.
3. Place the fish in a bowl; sprinkle sea salt, lemon juice and chilli oil and mix. Marinate for ten minutes.
4. Heat another non-stick pan; place the fish in it, cover and cook. Flip the fish cubes and cook on the other side too.
5. Transfer the potato mixture onto a serving bowl. Place the fish cubes over and serve hot.

073

STEAMED FISH WITH GINGER

Ingredients

2 whole pomfrets, scaled and cleaned
2 tablespoons thin strips of ginger
3 spring onion bulbs, sliced
Sea salt to taste
1 teaspoon sesame oil
10 spring onions with greens, sliced
1 teaspoon soy sauce
¼ teaspoon crushed black peppercorns
1 teaspoon chilli oil

Method

1. Heat sufficient water in the bottom half of a steamer. Place the perforated top over it.
2. Spread the spring onion bulb slices on the perforated top.
3. Make a few slits on the fish. Sprinkle a little sea salt over them and place them over the spring onions. Sprinkle half tablespoon ginger strips. Cover the steamer and let the fish steam till done.
4. Heat the sesame oil in a non-stick pan; add the spring onions with greens and sauté.
5. Add the soy sauce, remaining ginger strips, salt, crushed peppercorns, a one-fourth cup water and cook for three to four minutes.
6. Transfer the fish onto a serving plate. Pour the sauce over them. Drizzle chilli oil over them. Place the steamed sliced spring onion bulbs on top and serve immediately.

Noodles and Rice

074

FLAT NOODLES

Ingredients

400 grams flat noodles
2 lemongrass stalks, cut and crushed
1 inch lemongrass root, sliced
1 inch ginger, sliced
3 fresh red chillies, sliced
4-5 fresh coriander roots
2 tablespoons oil
2-3 spring onions, sliced
1 medium carrot, sliced
1 medium red capsicum, sliced
1 small broccoli, separated into florets
Salt to taste
50 grams bean curd (tofu), cut into triangles
1 tablespoon cornflour mixed in ¼ cup water
½ cup bean sprouts
1 tablespoon vinegar

Method

1. Heat two cups water in a non-stick wok. Add the lemongrass, lemongrass root, ginger and half the fresh red chillies. Add fresh coriander roots and cook for eight to ten minutes to make a flavourful stock. Strain the stock and set aside.
2. Cook the flat noodles in plenty of water till *al dente* (cooked but firm to the bite). Drain and cool.
3. Heat the oil in a non-stick wok. Add the spring onion, carrot, red capsicum and broccoli and sauté.
4. Add the reserved stock, noodles and salt and mix. Add the bean curd and cornflour mixture and let the mixture come to a boil.
5. Add the remaining fresh red chillies, bean sprouts and vinegar and mix.
6. Serve in a big bowl as one complete meal.

Image on the opposite page

075

CANTON-STYLE VEGETARIAN CHOWMEIN

Method

1. Heat three tablespoons oil in a non-stick pan. Spread the noodles evenly in the pan and let it cook on medium heat. Drizzle a little oil around the noodles.
2. When the noodles are crisp and golden on the underside, turn over and cook the other side similarly.When the noodles become golden on both sides, remove and drain on absorbent paper. Place them on a serving plate and set aside.
3. Mix the cornflour in one-fourth cup vegetable stock. Set aside.
4. Heat two tablespoons oil in another non-stick pan; add the spring onions and sauté.
5. Add the garlic paste to the spring onions and mix. Add the mushrooms and mix.
6. Drain the soya granules and add to the mushroom mixture. Add half cup vegetable stock and cook.
7. Add the soy sauce and mix and cook. Add the salt and crushed peppercorns, mix and cook.
8. Add the capsicums and mix well. Add the remaining stock and mix.
9. Add one tablespoon cornflour slurry and cook till the sauce thickens.
10. Pour this over the noodles and serve hot.

Ingredients

100 grams boiled noodles

5 tablespoons oil + for drizzling

2 teaspoons cornflour

1¼ cups Vegetable Stock (page 159)

3 spring onions, sliced vertically and roughly chopped

1 teaspoon garlic paste

6 button mushrooms, quartered

2 tablespoons soya granules, soaked

2 teaspoons light soy sauce

Salt to taste

Crushed black peppercorns to taste

½ medium red capsicum, cut into medium pieces

½ medium green capsicum, cut into medium pieces

½ medium yellow capsicum, cut into medium pieces

076

OODLES OF NOODLES

Ingredients

200 grams noodles, boiled
1 tablespoon oil
2 spring onions, diagonally sliced
4-5 French beans, blanched and diagonally sliced
½ cup sweetcorn kernels, boiled
1 small red capsicum, cut into strips
1 small yellow capsicum, cut into strips
2 teaspoons soy sauce
2 tablespoons tomato ketchup
2 teaspoons sweet chilli sauce
Salt to taste
2 stalks spring onion greens, chopped
¼ cup bean sprouts

Method

1. Heat the oil in a non-stick pan; add the spring onions and sauté for a minute. Add the French beans and sauté for a minute on high heat.
2. Add the corn kernels, boiled noodles, capsicums, soy sauce, tomato ketchup, sweet chilli sauce and salt and toss well.
3. Add the spring onion greens and bean sprouts and toss well.
4. Serve hot.

077

PEANUT BUTTER NOODLES

Ingredients

200 grams noodles, boiled
2 tablespoons peanut butter
7-8 spring onions with greens
1 inch ginger
6-7 garlic cloves
2 fresh red chillies
1 tablespoon oil
¼ cup dark soy sauce
2 tablespoons dark brown sugar
1 tablespoon vinegar
½ green capsicum, cut into thin strips
½ cup bean sprouts
¼ cup roasted peanuts

Method

1. Slice spring onion bulbs and chop spring onion greens. Set aside.
2. Chop together the ginger, garlic, fresh red chillies in a chopper. Set aside.
3. Heat the oil a non-stick wok; add the spring onions and sauté for half a minute. Add the ginger-garlic-red chillies mixture and sauté for half a minute.
4. Add the dark soy sauce and one-fourth cup water and stir.
5. Add the peanut butter and one-fourth cup water to the wok and stir to blend well. Add the brown sugar and vinegar and mix.
6. Add the noodles and capsicum and mix.
7. Add the spring onion greens along with bean sprouts. Toss well.
8. Add the roasted peanuts and mix. Serve hot.

078

NOODLES WITH MINCED SOYA

Method

1. Chop two onions and thickly slice the third onion. Mix cornflour in half cup vegetable stock till smooth. Slice spring onion bulbs and chop spring onion stems and greens. Reserve a little spring onion greens for garnishing.
2. Heat two tablespoons oil in a non-stick pan. Add the chopped onions and three teaspoons chopped garlic. Sauté till onions are light brown, add soya granules and mix. Add dark soy sauce, sweet chilli sauce and half cup vegetable stock and mix.
3. Add chopped spring onion stems and greens and further add half cup vegetable stock and mix. Add the crushed red chillies and mix. Add one teaspoon cornflour mixture and mix well. Adjust salt and add a little water and cook till the granules are completely done. Set aside.
4. Heat two tablespoons oil in another non-stick pan.
5. Add the thickly sliced onion and remaining garlic and sauté.
6. Add cabbage and mix. Add flat noodles, salt and half cup vegetable stock and mix.
7. Transfer the noodles onto a serving platter; pour the soya granule sauce over them, sprinkle the reserved spring onion greens and serve hot.

Ingredients

200 grams flat noodles, boiled
1 cup soya granules, soaked and drained
3 medium onions
1 teaspoon cornflour
2 cups Vegetable Stock (page 159)
2 spring onions with greens, chopped
4 tablespoons oil
4 teaspoons chopped garlic
2 teaspoons dark soy sauce
1 tablespoon sweet chilli sauce
½ teaspoon crushed red chillies
Salt to taste
¼ Chinese cabbage, shredded

079

SHANGHAI STEWED NOODLES

Ingredients

200 grams noodles
5 cups Vegetable Stock (page 159)
1 tablespoon oil
1 medium onion, sliced
6-8 garlic cloves, crushed
1 spring onion with greens, sliced
2 fresh button mushrooms, sliced
½ medium carrot, halved and sliced
½ medium green capsicum, cut into 1-inch pieces
¼ small cabbage, cut into 1-inch pieces
Salt to taste
½ teaspoon white pepper powder
1½ tablespoons cornflour
2 tablespoons chilli oil

Method

1. Place the noodles in a deep non-stick pan; add the vegetable stock and bring to a boil. Cook over a high heat for two minutes. Lower heat and simmer for four to five minutes, or until the noodles are almost cooked. Strain the noodles and reserve the stock.
2. Heat the oil in a non-stick wok; add the onion, garlic, spring onion with greens, mushrooms, carrot and capsicum and stir-fry for a few minutes. Add the salt, white pepper powder and cabbage and toss.
3. Add the noodles to the vegetables. Stir-fry for a minute and add the reserved vegetable stock and mix well.
4. Mix the cornflour with half a cup of water. Stir the cornflour mixture into the noodles. Cook, stirring frequently, over moderate heat for a couple of minutes or until the sauce thickens.
5. Drizzle the chilli oil and serve hot.

080

SPICY NOODLES IN A BOWL

Ingredients

For One Serving

50 grams noodles, boiled

2 teaspoons red chilli paste

2 teaspoons chilli oil

1 tablespoon oil

½ cup chopped onions

1 teaspoon chopped garlic

1 teaspoon chopped ginger

2 tablespoons soya granules, soaked in warm water and drained

Salt to taste

1 tablespoon honey

1 teaspoon vinegar

1 teaspoon sesame oil

2 spring onions, sliced

Method

1. Heat the oil in a non-stick wok. Add the onions, garlic and ginger and sauté. When the onions soften, add the soya granules and mix. Add two tablespoons water and mix.
2. Add the red chilli paste, salt and one-fourth cup water to the wok and mix. Add the honey and mix.
3. Add the vinegar to the soya mixture and mix. Add the sesame oil and mix. Keep warm.
4. Heat two cups water in a non-stick pan.
5. Add the boiled noodles to hot water and let them get heated through.
6. Add the salt and one teaspoon chilli oil to the noodles and mix.
7. Lift the noodles from hot water and place in a serving bowl.
8. Top the noodles with the soya granule mixture.
9. Garnish with sliced spring onions, drizzle the remaining chilli oil and serve immediately.

081

SWEET AND SOUR TOFU WITH NOODLES

Ingredients

100 grams silken bean curd (tofu), cut into 1-inch cubes

½ medium pineapple

¾ cup small cubes of fresh pineapple

1 cup pineapple juice

2 teaspoons vinegar

200 grams noodles, boiled

2 tablespoons oil

1 inch ginger, sliced

3-4 garlic cloves, sliced

1 medium onion, sliced

1 red capsicum, cut into ½-inch squares

3 teaspoons sugar

2 teaspoons hoisin sauce

Salt to taste

1 teaspoon cornflour

Method

1. Cut one-fourth of the whole pineapple, discard the head, scoop out the pulp and reserve the shell.
2. Heat the oil in a non-stick wok. Add tofu and sauté till light brown. Drain on absorbent paper and transfer into a bowl and set aside.
3. In the oil remaining in the wok, add the ginger, garlic and onion and sauté lightly. Add the pineapple cubes and sauté for half minute. Add the red capsicum and mix.
4. Add the sugar, hoisin sauce, pineapple juice and salt and mix.
5. Add the noodles and mix well. Mix the cornflour with two tablespoons water and add to the noodles. Cook till the sauce thickens. Add the vinegar and mix well.
6. Transfer the noodles into the pineapple shell, arrange the tofu pieces on it and serve hot.

082

PERFECT HAKKA NOODLES

Ingredients

400 grams noodles
Salt to taste
3 tablespoons oil
1 medium onion, sliced
6-8 French beans, sliced diagonally
1 medium carrot, cut into thin strips
¼ small cabbage, finely shredded
¼ teaspoon white pepper powder
1 tablespoon soy sauce
1 medium green capsicum, cut into thin strips
½ cup bean sprouts
1 tablespoon vinegar

Method

1. Heat seven cups water in a deep non-stick pan. Add salt and mix. Place a colander in it and put the noodles in the colander and cook. When the noodles are done, transfer the colander along with the noodles to another pan containing cold water.
2. Heat two tablespoons oil in a non-stick wok. Add onion, French beans, carrot and toss. Add cabbage and toss.
3. Remove the colander with the noodles from cold water and add the noodles to the vegetables.
4. Add remaining oil. Add salt, white pepper powder, soy sauce and toss on high heat.
5. Add capsicum, bean sprouts and vinegar and toss again. Serve hot.

083

VEGETABLE LO MEIN

Ingredients

250 grams spaghetti, boiled

2 medium carrots, cut diagonally into ½-inch pieces and blanched

4–6 button mushrooms, quartered

½ cup bean sprouts

2 teaspoons sesame oil

2-3 spring onion bulbs, quartered

1 tablespoon crushed garlic

1 tablespoon grated ginger

1 teaspoon hoisin sauce

Salt to taste

Crushed black peppercorns, to taste

Roughly chopped spring onion greens, for garnishing

Method

1. Heat the sesame oil in a non-stick pan. Add the spring onions and sauté till lightly browned.
2. Add the garlic and ginger and mix well. Add the carrot, mushrooms and mix well.
3. Add the spaghetti, hoisin sauce and salt and mix well. Add the crushed peppercorns and mix well. Add the bean sprouts and mix well. Add two tablespoons water and toss well. Cook for few minutes.
4. Transfer onto a serving plate, garnish with the spring onion greens and serve hot.

084

TOFU WITH STEWED NOODLES

Ingredients

50 grams bean curd (tofu)

1½ cups boiled noodles

1 medium potato, boiled, peeled and mashed

¼ cup crushed roasted peanuts

1 tablespoon grated ginger

1 medium onion, finely chopped

Salt to taste

1 tablespoon refined flour

2-3 tablespoons black sesame seeds

2 tablespoons oil + for shallow-frying

1 tablespoon crushed garlic

8-10 pak choi leaves

1 tablespoon red chilli sauce

Red chilli flakes, for garnishing

Finely chopped spring onion greens, for garnishing

Method

1. Place the potato in a bowl and grate the tofu into it. Add the peanuts, ginger, onion and salt and mix well. Add the refined flour and mix well. Divide the potato-tofu mixture into equal portions, shape them into balls, flatten to make tikkis.
2. Spread black sesame seeds in a plate. Roll the tikkis in the sesame seeds.
3. Heat sufficient oil in a non-stick pan. Shallow-fry the potato-tofu tikkis, flip over and cook till golden and crisp on both the sides. Drain on absorbent paper and set aside.
4. Heat one tablespoon oil in another non-stick pan. Add the garlic and sauté for half a minute. Add the pak choi, half cup water and salt and mix well. Cook till the pak choi is done. Set aside.
5. Heat remaining oil in a third non-stick pan.
6. Add the noodles, red chilli sauce, one-fourth cup water and salt and mix well. Cook till the noodles are heated through.
7. Transfer the stewed noodles on a serving plate; sprinkle some red chilli flakes on top and garnish with the spring onion greens. Place the pak choi mixture and potato-tofu tikkis by the side of the noodle and serve immediately.

085

CHICKEN AND RICE NOODLE STIR-FRIED

Ingredients

400 grams boneless chicken breasts, cut into thin strips

200 grams rice noodles

4 tablespoons oil

Salt to taste

A few fresh coriander sprigs, roughly chopped

Juice of ½ lemon

2 spring onion bulbs, sliced

6-8 garlic cloves, finely chopped

1 tablespoon dark soy sauce

1 tablespoon oyster sauce

½ teaspoon white pepper powder

1 medium green capsicum, cut into thin strips

Method

1. Soak the rice noodles in sufficient boiling water for five minutes. Drain and cool.
2. Heat two tablespoons oil in a non-stick wok.
3. Add the noodles and salt and sauté till heated through. Add a little water, fresh coriander sprigs, lemon juice and mix gently. Transfer into a bowl.
4. Heat the remaining oil in the same wok. Add the spring onion bulbs and garlic and sauté for one minute.
5. Add the chicken and stir-fry. Add the dark soy sauce and oyster sauce and mix and cook till the chicken is done.
6. Add the white pepper powder and cook. Add the green capsicum and mix.
7. Place the rice noodles on a serving plate; top with the chicken and serve hot.

086

CHILLI FISH IN NOODLE NEST

Ingredients

400 grams basa fish fillets, cut into 1-inch cubes
2-3 fresh red chillies, diagonally sliced
200 grams boiled noodles
2 tablespoons oil + for deep-frying
Salt to taste
1 teaspoon crushed black peppercorns
1 egg
½ cup cornflour
1 tablespoon chopped garlic
1 inch ginger, finely chopped
1 medium onion, quartered and layers separated
1 medium green capsicum, cut into diamonds
2 teaspoons dark soy sauce
1 cup Fish Stock (page 159)

Method

1. Heat sufficient oil in a wok.
2. Place the fish in a bowl; add the salt, half teaspoon crushed peppercorns, egg and four tablespoons cornflour and mix well. Deep-fry the fish on medium heat till golden brown and crisp. Drain on absorbent paper and set aside.
3. Place the noodles in a bowl. Add three tablespoons cornflour and mix lightly.
4. To make the noodle nest, spread a portion of the noodles in a fine sieve; place another fine sieve on the noodles and press. Lower the sieves along with the noodles into the hot oil and deep-fry till golden and crisp. Drain on absorbent paper. Set aside. Make few more noodle nests with the remaining noodles.
5. Heat two tablespoons oil in a non-stick wok. Add the garlic, ginger and fresh red chillies and sauté for thirty seconds.

6. Add the onion, capsicum and toss well. Add the salt, remaining crushed peppercorns, soy sauce and fish stock and mix. Bring to a boil.
7. Mix the remaining cornflour with two tablespoons water to make a thick slurry.
8. Add the slurry to the sauce, mix and cook till it thickens. Add the fried fish and toss well.
9. Transfer equal portions of the fish mixture into the noodle nests and serve immediately.

087

BUTTER GARLIC VEGETABLE FRIED RICE

Ingredients

3 cups cooked rice
3 tablespoons butter
7-8 green garlic cloves, finely chopped
2 tablespoons garlic paste
8-10 green garlic stalks, finely chopped
2 tablespoons chopped French beans
2 tablespoons grated cabbage
2 tablespoons grated cauliflower
2 tablespoons grated carrot
½ cup chopped onions
Salt to taste

Method

1. Heat the butter in a non-stick wok; add the green garlic and onions and sauté.
2. Add the French beans, cabbage, cauliflower and carrot and mix well.
3. Add the salt and cooked rice. Add one-fourth cup water and garlic paste and mix well.
4. Add the green garlic stalks and mix well. Cook for two to three minutes.
5. Transfer into a serving bowl and serve hot.

088

SICHUAN VEGETABLE FRIED RICE

Ingredients

1½ cups rice, soaked
1 medium carrot, finely chopped
4-6 French beans, finely chopped
2 spring onions with greens, finely chopped
3 tablespoons oil
3-4 dried red chillies, broken
4-6 garlic cloves, finely chopped
1 inch ginger, finely chopped
1 tablespoon red chilli paste
¼ teaspoon white pepper powder
Salt to taste
1 tablespoon vinegar

Method

1. Boil four cups water in a deep non-stick pan; add the rice and cook until just cooked. Drain well and cool.
2. Heat the oil in a non-stick wok; add the red chillies, garlic, ginger and spring onions, reserving some for garnishing, and sauté for one minute.
3. Add the carrot and French beans and continue to sauté for a minute. Add the red chilli paste, white pepper powder and salt and mix well.
4. Add the rice and cook on high heat for a minute or until the rice is heated through, tossing continuously.
5. Add the vinegar and mix well. Serve hot, garnished with the reserved spring onion greens.

Ingredients

1 cup short grained rice, soaked

2 tablespoons olive oil

2 medium onions, roughly chopped

2 medium carrots, cut into medium-sized pieces

1½ tablespoons grated ginger

1½ tablespoons grated garlic

1 teaspoon soy sauce

3 cups Vegetable Stock (page 159)

½ teaspoon black pepper powder

1 teaspoon sesame oil

089

CHINESE-STYLE VEGETABLE CLAY POT RICE

Method

1. Heat two tablespoons olive oil in a non-stick pan. Add onions and sauté.
2. Add carrots and sauté. Add ginger and garlic and sauté.
3. Add soy sauce and vegetable stock and mix. Drain and add rice and pepper powder and mix. Cover and cook on low heat till half done.
4. Transfer the mixture into a claypot. Add sesame oil. Cover and cook for twenty-five to thirty minutes or till the rice is completely cooked and ensure that it is still moist.
5. Serve hot.

090

BURNT GINGER RICE

Ingredients

2 cups cooked short-grained or Kolam rice
4 inches ginger, finely sliced
4 tablespoons oil
2 spring onion bulbs, cut into thick round slices
Salt to taste
¼ teaspoon white pepper powder
8 garlic cloves, chopped
10 broccoli florets
2 teaspoons cornflour mixed with 2 tablespoons water

Method

1. Heat two tablespoons oil in a non-stick wok. Add the ginger and sauté on high heat till crisp and burnt. Add the spring onion bulbs and toss.
2. Add the rice, salt and white pepper powder and toss. Transfer into a bowl.
3. Heat the remaining oil in the same wok, add the garlic and toss lightly. Add the broccoli, a little water and salt and toss. Add cornflour mixture and mix.
4. Add the rice mixture and mix lightly.
5. Serve hot.

6. Add the pak choi mixture to the mixture in the wok. Add the cornflour mixture and cook till the sauce thickens. Add the vinegar and mix again.
7. Add the chopped mushrooms and mix.
8. Place the rice in a clay pot.
9. Pour the mixture over the rice in the clay pot. Cover and place it in the preheated oven and bake for fifteen to twenty minutes.
10. Serve hot.

091

CLAY POT RICE

Ingredients

2 cups cooked rice

2-3 pak choi leaves, hand torn

1 star anise

6-8 dried mushrooms

Salt to taste

2 tablespoons oil

1 medium onion, thickly sliced

1 tablespoon chopped ginger

5-6 garlic cloves, chopped

5-6 button mushrooms, quartered

100 grams bean curd (tofu), cut into ½-inch cubes

2 teaspoons soy sauce

2 teaspoons hoisin sauce

1 teaspoon white pepper powder

2 tablespoons cornflour mixed with 4 tablespoons water

1 tablespoon vinegar

Method

1. Pour two cups water in a deep non-stick pan; add pak choi, star anise, dried mushrooms and salt and cook for four to five minutes.
2. Heat the oil in a non-stick wok. Add the onion, ginger and garlic and sauté for two to three minutes.
3. Preheat the oven to 200°C/400°F/Gas Mark 6.
4. Add the button mushrooms and tofu to the wok and toss. Add the soy sauce and hoisin sauce and mix. Add the white pepper powder and mix.
5. Remove the star anise from the pak choi mixture and discard. Remove the dried mushrooms; chop them and set aside.

092

LOTUS LEAF RICE

Ingredients

3 cups cooked rice
4 lotus leaves
2 tablespoons oil
2 spring onions, diagonally sliced
1 teaspoon chopped garlic
1 fresh red chilli, finely chopped
4 button mushrooms, sliced
4-5 water chestnuts, sliced
1 cup Vegetable Stock (page 159)
2 tablespoons frozen green peas
Salt to taste

Method

1. Heat the oil in a non-stick pan; add the spring onions and garlic and sauté.
2. Add the fresh red chilli and button mushrooms and mix. Add the water chestnuts and half cup vegetable stock and cook for a couple of minutes.
3. Add the green peas and mix.
4. Add the cooked rice and the remaining vegetable stock and mix. Add the salt and mix. Remove from the heat.
5. Trim the stems of the lotus leaves.
6. Place some rice mixture in the centre of each lotus leaf and fold the leaf from all four sides to make a parcel.
7. Bring to boil three cups water in a deep non-stick pan.
8. Keep a bamboo steamer in the deep pan with boiling water. Place the parcels, folded side facing downwards, in the steamer, and cover the steamer. Cover the pan also and steam for five minutes.

9. You can serve it in the steamer itself. Or take the parcel out and place on a serving plate, folded side facing downwards. Cut the leaf in a cross from the centre and open. Serve immediately.

093

CHINESE TOMATO EGG-DROP RICE

Ingredients

3 cups cooked Kolam rice
2 medium tomatoes, chopped
4 tablespoons tomato ketchup
6 eggs
3 tablespoons oil
2 tablespoon chopped garlic
4 spring onion bulbs, chopped
Salt to taste
½ teaspoon white pepper powder to taste
5 stalks spring onion greens, chopped
4 teaspoons vinegar
2 teaspoons soy sauce
2 tablespoons cornflour
Few fresh coriander sprigs for garnishing

Method

1. Boil four eggs. Cool, peel and halve them and discard yolks. Roughly chop the egg whites and set aside. Break the remaining two eggs, discard the yolks and place the egg whites in a bowl. Beat the egg whites and set aside.
2. Heat the oil in a non-stick wok. Add the garlic and sauté till burnt. Add the spring onion bulbs and toss. Add the rice, salt and one-fourth teaspoon white pepper powder, toss again and cook for one minute. Add the chopped egg whites and spring onion greens and mix well. Add three teaspoons vinegar. Mix well and remove from heat.
3. Heat two cups water in another non-stick wok. Add the tomato ketchup and tomatoes and bring it to a boil.
4. Adjust the salt and add the soy sauce and remaining white pepper powder. Mix well.
5. Mix cornflour with four tablespoons water and add to the pan along with the remaining vinegar. Mix well and bring to boil. Add the beaten egg whites and mix well. Remove from heat.

6. Place the rice in a serving dish and pour tomato-egg drop sauce on top. Garnish with a few fresh coriander sprigs and serve hot.

Accompaniments

094

PICKLED CABBAGE

Ingredients

1 medium cabbage, roughly shredded
1 tablespoon oil
2 teaspoons Sichuan sauce
1 teaspoon soy sauce
Salt to taste
2 teaspoons sugar
1 teaspoon vinegar

Method

1. Heat the oil in a non-stick pan; add the cabbage, Sichuan sauce and soy sauce and mix well. Add the salt and mix again. Add the sugar and vinegar and mix well. Remove from the heat and transfer into a bowl.
2. Refrigerate for three to four hours and serve as an accompaniment.

Image on the opposite page

095

TOFU DIP WITH PEANUTS

Ingredients

50 grams silken bean curd (tofu), cut into cubes

1 tablespoon peanut butter

1 medium green capsicum, cut into fingers

1 medium red capsicum, cut into fingers

8-12 broccoli florets, blanched

1 medium carrot, cut into fingers and blanched

2 spring onion with greens, roughly chopped

1 teaspoon garlic paste

2 teaspoons red chilli sauce

½ teaspoon soy sauce

Thin strips of spring onion greens for garnishing

Method

1. Arrange the green and red capsicum fingers, broccoli florets and carrot fingers on a serving platter.
2. Place the spring onions in a mixer jar. Add the tofu, garlic paste, peanut butter, red chilli sauce and soy sauce and blend till smooth.
3. Transfer into a serving bowl, garnish with thin strips of spring onion green and serve with the vegetables arranged on the serving platter.

096

CRACKLING SPINACH

Ingredients

For One Portion

3 medium bunches (250 grams each) spinach

Oil for deep-frying

Salt to taste

1 tablespoon sugar

1 teaspoon crushed red chillies

1 tablespoon toasted sesame seeds

1 tablespoon sesame oil

Method

1. Trim the stems and use only the spinach leaves. Wash them under running water. Dry well. Stack them one on top of the other, fold and shred finely.
2. Heat sufficient oil in a wok; add the shredded spinach leaves and deep-fry till crisp and dark green in colour. Drain on absorbent paper.
3. Transfer onto a serving plate. Sprinkle salt, sugar, crushed red chillies and toasted sesame seeds. Drizzle sesame oil and serve immediately.

Sweets

097

TOFFEE APPLE

Ingredients

4 medium apples, seeded and cut each into 8 thick slices

1 cup refined flour

4 tablespoons oil + for deep-frying

2 tablespoons honey + for drizzling

½ teaspoon baking powder

2 cups caster sugar

1 tablespoon toasted sesame seeds

Method

1. In a bowl, whisk together the refined flour and four tablespoons oil with one-fourth cup chilled water till smooth. Add two tablespoons honey and whisk again.
2. Add the baking powder to the batter and mix.
3. Cook together the sugar and one-fourth cup water in a non-stick pan till it attains one-string consistency.
4. Heat sufficient oil in a kadai.
5. Dip the apple slices in the batter and deep-fry till crisp. Drain on absorbent paper.
6. Dip the fried apple slices in the sugar syrup and place on a serving plate.
7. Drizzle the honey and sprinkle sesame seeds over them and serve immediately.

Image on the opposite page

098

SWEET WONTONS

Ingredients

8 Wonton Wrappers (page 159)

¼ cup roasted peanuts

4-5 seedless dates, roughly chopped

2 tablespoons brown sugar

½ cup grated fresh coconut

1 tablespoon toasted white sesame seeds + for sprinkling

8 teaspoons cornflour slurry

Oil for deep-frying

Honey, for drizzling

Black sesame seeds, for sprinkling

Method

1. Place the roasted peanuts in a blender jar. Add the dates and blend well. Add the brown sugar and blend again.
2. Add the fresh coconut and continue to blend till well mixed. Transfer the mixture into a bowl. Add one tablespoon sesame seeds and mix well.
3. Place the wonton wrappers on a worktop; place a portion of the peanut mixture in the centre of each wrapper, apply one teaspoon cornflour slurry on the edges, fold over to make triangular parcels and seal the edges.
4. Heat sufficient oil in a wok.
5. Gently slide the wontons into the hot oil and deep-fry till crisp and golden. Drain on absorbent paper.
6. Arrange the wontons on a serving platter, drizzle the honey, sprinkle some white and black sesame seeds and serve immediately.

099

CHOCOLATE SPRING ROLLS

Ingredients

Spring Roll Wrappers

1 cup + 3 tablespoons refined flour

Nougat

100 grams roughly chopped milk chocolate

2 tablespoons roughly chopped pistachios

2 tablespoons roughly chopped almonds

½ cup grain sugar

Oil for deep-frying

Method

1. For the wrappers, add sufficient water to one cup refined flour in a bowl and knead into a semi-soft dough. Set aside.
2. For the nougat, heat sugar in a non-stick pan. Sprinkle some water and once the sugar starts to caramelise, switch off the heat and add chopped nuts and mix well.
3. Spread the mixture evenly on silicon sheet and allow to cool. Crush lightly and mix with the chocolate.
4. Add a little water to three tablespoons of refined flour in another bowl to make a thick slurry and set aside.
5. Divide the dough into equal portions and shape them into balls. Shape the balls into a thin round disc and place a portion of stuffing on one side. Apply slurry on the edge of the disc and roll tightly.
6. Heat sufficient oil in a kadai and deep-fry the prepared spring rolls till golden brown and crisp on both the sides. Drain on absorbent paper and serve hot.

100

DAARSAAN

Ingredients

16-20 Wonton Wrappers (page 159)
Oil for deep-frying
1 tablespoon butter
¼ cup sugar
¼ cup honey
2 tablespoons sesame seeds, toasted
2 tablespoons icing sugar

Method

1. Cut the wonton wrappers into quarter inch thick strips.
2. Heat sufficient oil in a wok; deep-fry the wonton strips for one minute, or until crisp and golden brown. Drain on absorbent paper and transfer to a shallow serving dish. Keep warm.
3. Heat butter in a non-stick pan with one tablespoon of water and sugar. Cook until sugar melts and turns a light golden brown. Lower heat and stir in the honey. Pour the hot sauce over the fried wontons. Sprinkle with toasted sesame seeds and icing sugar and serve warm.

ANNEXURE

Chicken Stock

Boil 200 grams chicken bones in water for 5 minutes. Drain and discard water. Boil blanched bones with a roughly chopped carrot, celery stalk, leek, 2-3 parsley stalks, 6-7 black peppercorns, 5-6 cloves, 1 bay leaf and 10 cups of water. Remove any scum which rises to the surface and replace it with more cold water. Simmer for at least 1 hour. Remove from heat, strain, cool and store in a refrigerator till further use.

Coconut Milk

Process 1 cup grated fresh coconut in a blender with ¼ cup warm water. Pass the ground coconut through a piece of muslin or strainer pressing firmly to extract all the juice, or first milk. Add a ¼ cup of warm water to the strained coconut to get the second, thinner milk from the same solids.

Fish Stock

Place 200 grams fish bones, including head, skin and any unutilised portions of fish, in a non- stick pan with 5 cups of water, 1 sliced medium onion, 1 sliced large fresh button mushroom, 2-3 inches celery stalk, cut into ½-inch pieces, 1 bay leaf and 4-6 peppercorns. Bring to a boil, remove any scum, which rises to the surface and simmer for 15 minutes. Remove from heat and strain. Discard solids. Use immediately.

Vegetable Stock

Peel, wash and chop 1 onion, ½ medium carrot, 2-3 inches celery stalk and 2-3 garlic cloves. Place in a pan with 1 bay leaf, 5-6 peppercorns, 2-3 cloves and 5 cups of water and bring to a boil. Lower heat and simmer for 15 minutes and strain. Cool and store in a refrigerator till further use.

Wonton Wrappers

Knead 2 cups of refined flour with ½ cup warm water to make a firm dough. Roll the dough into a large thin square sheet, about 1 mm thick. Cut into 3-inch squares and use as required.

GLOSSARY

English	Hindi
Almond	Badam
Apple	Saeb
Apricot	Khubani
Banana leaf	Kele ka patta
Bean sprouts	Ankurit moong
Black pepper powder	Kali mirch powder
Black peppercorns	Kali mirch
Bread	Double roti
Brinjal/Eggplant/Aubergine	Baingan
Broccoli	Hari phoolgobhi
Butter	Makkhan
Buttermilk	Chaas
Button mushroom	Khumbh/dhingri
Cabbage	Pattagobhi
Carrot	Gajar
Cashewnut	Kaju
Cauliflower	Phoolgobhi
Cherry tomatoes	Chhote tamatar
Chicken mince/Minced chicken	Murgh ka keema
Cinnamon	Dalchini
Coconut	Nariyal
Coconut milk	Nariyal ka doodh
Corn kernels	Makai ke dane
Cottage cheese	Paneer/chhena
Crushed black peppercorns	Kuti hui kali mirch
Cucumber	Kakdi/kheera
Dates	Khajur
Dried red chillies	Sookhi lal mirch
Egg	Anda
Egg white	Ande ki safedi
French beans	Farsi
Fresh coriander leaves	Hara dhania
Fresh mint leaves	Pudina
Fresh parsely	Ajmod
Fresh red chilli	Tazi lal mirch
Garlic	Lehsun
Garlic paste	Lehsun ka paste
Ginger	Adrak
Ginger paste	Adrak ka paste
Green capsicum	Hari shimla mirch
Green chilli	Hari mirch
Green peas	Hare matar
Honey	Shahad
Indian salmon	Rawas machli
Lemon	Nimboo
Lemongrass stalk	Hari chai ki patti
Lemon juice	Nimboo ka ras
Lemon zest/Lemon rind	Nimboo ka chilka
Long beans	Chawli
Lotus roots	Kamal Kakdi/Nadru
Milk	Doodh
Oil	Tel
Olive oil	Jaitun ka tel
Olives (black, green)	Jaitun (kale, hare)
Onion	Pyaaz
Onion seeds	Kalonji
Orange juice	Santre ka ras
Palm sugar	Taad ki cheeni
Peanuts	Moongphali
Pineapple	Annanas
Pistachio	Pista
Pomfret	Halva/Saranga/Chandwa/ Poplait machli
Potato	Aloo
Prawn	Jheenga
Pumpkin seeds	Kaddu ke beej
Red capsicum	Lal shimla mirch
Red chilli flakes/ Crushed red chillies	Kooti hui sookhi lal mirch
Red chilli powder	Lal mirch powder
Refined flour	Maida
Rice	Chawal
Salt	Namak
Sea salt	Samudri namak
Sesame oil	Til ka tel
Sesame seeds (black, white)	Til (kale, safed)
Shallots	Chhote pyaaz
Spinach	Palak
Spring onion	Hara pyaaz
Spring onion greens	Hare pyaaz ki patti
Star anise	Phool chakri/badiyan
Sugar	Cheeni/shakkar
Sunflower seeds	Surajmukhi ke beej
Tea leaves	Chai ke patte
Tofu/Beancurd	Soya paneer
Tomato	Tamatar
Vinegar	Sirka
Walnut/Walnut kernels	Akhrot
Water chestnuts	Singhada
White vinegar	Safed sirka
Yellow capsicum	Pili shimla mirch